YOU BE THE JUDGE

THE STRANGE AND THE SUPERNATURAL

YOU BE THE JUDGE

THE STRANGE AND THE SUPERNATURAL

BRIAN PEACHMENT
Lecturer in Drama, Middleton
St. George College of Education

Edward Arnold

First published 1972
by Edward Arnold (Publishers) Ltd
41 Maddox Street
London WIR OAN

ISBN 0 7131 1663 3

Printed in Great Britain by
Fletcher & Son Ltd, Norwich

CONTENTS

ACKNOWLEDGMENTS

The Publisher's thanks are due to the following for permission to use copyright material:

Neville Spearman Ltd for 'Can You Convince me that this Isn't a Dream' from Albert K. Bender's *Flying Saucers and the Three Men*; the Rev. J. A. Carruth for 'The Savage Monster'; Gordon Collier for 'Four Fingers' from *Strange Horizons*; the University of Colorado and Bantam Books for Case 29 from *Scientific Study of Unidentified Flying Objects*; 'Fate' Magazine for 'Duel by Witchcraft' by Major C. Court-Treatt as told to Helen Hunger in *The Strange and the Unknown*, and 'The Priest and the Saucer' by the Rev. Father R. Dean Johnson in *Strange Fate*; Routledge & Kegan Paul Ltd for 'Identi-kit for a Monster' and 'The Thrills of the Chase' from Tim Dinsdale's *Loch Ness Monster*; Hutchinson Publishing Group Ltd for 'The Unquiet Tomb', 'Pup-petry' and 'Village of Walking Dead' from Valentine Dyall's *Unsolved Mysteries*; Martin Gardner for 'The Controversy' from *Fads and Fallacies in the Name of Science*; The Bodley Head for 'The Haunted Rest House' from *Ju-Ju and Justice in Nigeria* by Frank Hives and Gascoigne Lumley; Curtis Brown Ltd for 'The Mystery of the Mary Celeste' from J. G. Lockhart's *The Mary Celeste and Other Strange Tales of the Sea*; The New American Library Inc., N.Y. for 'From Mars with . . .' from Coral E. Lorenzen's *Flying Saucers*; George G. Harrap for 'Bad Things on Black Saturday' from James H. Neal's *Ju-Ju in my Life*; Dennis Dobson Ltd for 'Ordeal by Fire' by E. F. Russell in *Great World Mysteries*; Penguin Books Ltd for 'The Eagle has Landed' from Peter Ryan's *The Invasion of the Moon 1969*; Eric Stevens for 'The Great Monster Hunt' and 'Nessie Baffles the Boffins' (ITN News); Gerald Duckworth & Co. Ltd. for 'The Phantom Flyer' from D. J. West's *Psychical Research Today*; The *Daily Telegraph* for Vivian Craddock Williams's 'Sadly Among the Turnip

Lanterns'; Souvenir Press Ltd for 'Jungle Dentistry' from Harold B. Wright's *Witness to Witchcraft* and Mrs Constance Whyte for 'Out of the Water' from *More than a Legend*.

We would also like to thank the following for their kind permission to reproduce the photographs in this book:

Radio Times Hulton Picture Library (18, 34, 36, 64); Barnaby's Picture Library (41); Camera Press (79, 95, 133, 151, 152); Society for Psychical Research (87); Tim Dinsdale (128–9); John Sanders (153–4).

The cover photograph is by courtesy of the U.S. Air Force.

INTRODUCTION

Most of the material in this book consists of factual writings on the strange and the supernatural taken from journals, newspapers, and other non-literary sources as well as books, written by those who accept para-normal events at their face value and also by those of their critics who seek a more natural explanation.

The extracts are set in an editorial framework which includes questions and pointers designed to stimulate thought and discussion in the classroom. The book will have served its purpose well if the next time you see a ghost, a flying saucer or the Loch Ness monster, you consider all the natural possibilities before rushing off to tell your friends hair-raising tales of your contact with the occult. In dealing with the supernatural, as in all other areas of human experience you must examine the evidence carefully and then make up your own mind. Read on, therefore, and YOU BE THE JUDGE.

STRANGE UNSOLVED MYSTERIES

Throughout history there have been events so mysterious and baffling that all attempts to find a natural explanation for them have failed. Among the many examples of the strange and the supernatural one of the most curious is the poltergeist. Poltergeist is a German word meaning noisy ghost and is applied to inanimate objects which suddenly, and for no apparent reason, take on a disturbing life of their own.

In 1927, a poltergeist invaded the London home of an eighty-six-year-old invalid, Mr Henry Robinson.* Mr Robinson lived at 8 Eland Road, Battersea, with his twenty-seven-year-old son, his daughters Kate and Lillah, and his married daughter, Mrs George Perkins, who had a fourteen-year-old son, Peter. Their reign of terror began on November 29th 1927, and continued into the new year. A conservatory at the back of the house became the target for the first attacks: potatoes, pieces of soda, coal, pebbles, red hot cinders, and pennies showered on to the roof breaking some of the panes of glass. The objects when weighed were all found to be more than usually heavy. The police were called in but a thorough inspection of the house and its surroundings yielded no clue as to the origin of the strange missiles. Inside the house chairs paraded in single file down the stairs, crockery fell off the shelves, heavy furniture tumbled over, weird banging sounds were heard in all the rooms, and the window panes were continually being shattered. When Mrs Perkins tried to lay the table for dinner one evening the chairs repeatedly flew up and swept the crockery on to the carpet. When at last she managed to

* *Unsolved Mysteries*, by Valentine Dyall.

lay the table, it gave a wild lurch which sent the plates of food crashing to the floor. There were almost one hundred of these strange occurrences which eventually broke the health of Mr Henry Robinson and threatened that of his son. With their nerves badly worn, the family finally managed to collect their belongings together and moved to a new address as far away as possible from their strange 'house where the furniture danced'.

It is not only private houses which are singled out by poltergeists for their strange activities, they have also been known to frequent business offices. Mr George Wheeler, a court reporter, rented a third floor, three roomed office at 1904 Franklin Street, Oakland, on San Francisco Bay, California.* His encounter with a poltergeist began in 1964 when his office was wrecked by unseen forces. Telephones and typewriters jumped off the desks, a heavy cabinet repeatedly fell over, a typewriter top leaped off the machine and flew across the room crashing into the opposite wall. A light beside the telephone kept flashing, indicating that a caller was on the line, but when the receiver was picked up no one answered from the other end. Engineers carefully checked the telephone system, but no fault could be found. The return-action springs on the electric typewriters were continually becoming twisted or lost their springiness altogether. Springs in the typewriters loaned to Mr Wheeler while his own machines were being repaired also became entangled or failed to spring back when required. The manager of the typewriter repair firm confessed his amazement: he had never experienced anything quite like it before. The springs normally lasted the life of the typewriter but his mechanics had to fit a hundred new springs to Mr Wheeler's machines in only a few days. The office staff moved to another office on the second floor, but the poltergeist followed them. The metal top on one of the typewriters jumped off its machine, flew out of the window, and fell on to the roof of a car parked in the street below. Poltergeist activity usually follows a pattern: the disturbances become more and more devastating, reach a climax and then fizzle out. Such an ending came for Mr Wheeler on June 17 when an eight-foot high wooden cabinet containing office equipment fell over scattering paper and office materials about the room, creating havoc in his office. The worst was over, the poltergeist activity stopped soon afterwards leaving Mr Wheeler and his staff to carry on their work undisturbed.

One of the strangest cases of objects taking on a life of their own is found in the bewildering story of *The Flying Coffins of Barbados* or, as it is known in the following account:

THE UNQUIET TOMB

In the midday heat of April 18th 1820, six silent men came down from a headland on the island of Barbados, their eyes

* *Poltergeist Wrecks Business Office*, by Jim Hazlewood. Article in *Strange Fate*.

downcast, their expressions a mixture of horror and bewilderment.

To waiting townspeople they said little: but before many hours had passed three of them had put on paper detailed accounts of a series of events so strange and uncanny that even today they remain one of the world's great unsolved mysteries—the enigma of the unquiet tomb. . . .

If you go to the island today you can see for yourself that the lower walls of the Elliott vault are solid rock, hewn out of the hillside above beautiful Oistin's Bay.

Warm winds blowing in from the blue Caribbean set tropical blooms nodding in the little churchyard. Birds sing lustily in the eaves of the parish church, and you walk between weather-worn headstones which face only the open sea.

It would be hard to imagine a less appropriate setting for the odd, the eerie, the totally inexplicable. . . .

There are other vaults in the cemetery of Christ Church, but the Elliott tomb alone stands empty and neglected. The entrance is unbarred and if you venture down the short flight of stone steps you will find only casual rubbish and a few hardy weeds. It has been abandoned and shunned for more than a century: it will almost certainly remain deserted until its heavy coral rock masonry has crumbled away. For there is evidence that within these walls there can be no rest for the dead.

The vault was built in 1724 to receive the remains of the Hon. John Elliott. But curiously enough there is no record that he was ever interred there, and it seems probable that it remained unused for the surprising period of eighty-three years.

The church register shows that the first burial there took place on July 31st 1807, when the body of Mrs Thomasina Goddard was laid to rest. About a year later the vault appears to have passed to new owners, the Chase family, and on February 22nd 1808, the tiny coffin of the infant Mary Anna Maria Chase was carried down the stone steps.

On July 6th 1812, another daughter, Dorcas Chase—apparently an adult—was interred in the vault, to be followed only thirty-four days later, on August 9th, by the father himself, the Hon. Thomas Chase.

At this funeral—the fourth at the vault—many leading citizens were among the mourners. They stood in a silent semicircle while burly Negro servants put their shoulders to the ponderous slab of blue Devonshire marble which sealed the entrance.

Seconds later the superstitious Negroes were fleeing downhill in terror. The startled mourners hurried to the entrance—then cried out in anger and dismay.

Some violent force had been at work within. The coffins of Mrs Goddard and little Mary Chase appeared to have been lifted from their places and thrown against the walls. The smaller one stood on end in the north-east corner, head downward; the larger lay askew, several feet from its proper place. The coffin of Dorcas Chase alone was undisturbed.

The outraged relatives' first thoughts were that negro grave-robbers had broken in. But when a thorough examination revealed that nothing had been removed from the tomb they fell back on the theory that spiteful or mischievous labourers were responsible for this strange desecration.

After some indignant discussion the funeral service went on, the four coffins were placed in order and the vault was securely closed.

Naturally, the Chase family kept the whole affair as quiet as possible, and the Negroes' story gained little credence except among their own people. Four years later, when once again a melancholy procession wound its way up the hill to the Elliott vault, the affair was all but forgotten.

The date was September 25th 1816; the deceased—another infant, Samuel Brewster Ames. Again the interior was found in crazy confusion. . . .

This time it was impossible to hush-up stories of 'the tomb that tries to vomit up its dead'. The relatives once more blamed 'bad Negroes', but the Negroes hotly denied the charge and wailed that 'jumbies' or 'doppies', traditional evil spirits, were responsible.

For the next two months the sinister affair monopolised Barbadian conversation. And on November 17th, when the body of Mr Samuel Brewster was carried to the vault, curious crowds flocked to watch the interment from a respectful distance.

Five apprehensive Negroes heaved aside the great slab of marble. They bolted when the same macabre chaos was revealed within. A curious fact is that on this occasion Mrs Goddard's coffin—the oldest of the five, and the only one of purely wooden construction—alone was undisturbed. After nine years in the vault it was in an advanced state of decay.

In tropical areas where destructive insects abound, wood offers poor protection. Barbadians had learned this in early settlement days, and the vast majority of their nineteenth-century coffins had an outer casing of lead. The fact that the single all-wood coffin in the vault had remained in position while its heavier neighbours were scattered and up-ended was to prove the main stumbling-block for the legion of investigators who later sought a natural explanation for the phenomenon.

Thousands of awed sightseers trooped uphill to view 'the haunted tomb'. In the next few days excitement mounted throughout the island to such an extent that officialdom could no longer ignore the subject.

Lord Combermere, Governor of Barbados, was a stern, practical man—a soldier and a disciplinarian with a healthy contempt for superstition. He listened to reports of the affair, interviewed witnesses, and decided to attend the next interment at the vault. On July 17 1819, accompanied by three aides, he followed the coffin of a woman named Thomasina Clarke to the churchyard on the headland.

For the fourth time the contents of the tomb were found in utter confusion: the unknown force had been at work again. . . .

The watching crowd fell back, suddenly hushed. This time no cries came from the mourners—they were too awed, too bewildered. But Combermere—who had fought alongside Wellington in the Peninsular Wars—was not so easily daunted. He strode forward and descended into the half-light. For about a minute he poked about with his cane amid the disordered coffins, then he called for a lantern.

Others took courage and joined him in the vault. By the flickering light they examined every inch of the rock floor, walls, and roof. No trace of a subterranean passage or secret entrance could be found; not even a crack.

Combermere pursed his lips and walked up the stairs deep in thought. While the coffins were replaced he paced up and down in the strong sunlight, perhaps wondering what strategy the Iron Duke would adopt in a situation like this.

His soldier's logic must have told him that some trick was being played on the entire population. There was one sure way to put an end to it: he would make certain that no living creature could enter the tomb without leaving obvious traces.

After the mourners and the curious spectators had left he ordered a few trusted friends and officials to fetch tools and materials. Mrs Goddard's coffin by now had fallen to pieces. It was tied together in a bundle and propped against the rear wall.

The floor of the vault was carefully covered with fine coral sand, so that the slightest movement would leave its mark. The marble slab was manhandled into position and secured with cement.

The Elliott tomb was now hermetically sealed.

Before the cement dried, the Governor took his signet ring and made several impressions. Others in the party added various private marks. They walked downhill confident that no human agency could interfere with the six coffins and go undetected.

Something close on panic now gripped the Negro population, and the Europeans speculated widely on what would be found the next time the tomb was opened.

On April 18th 1820—exactly nine months after Thomasina Clarke's burial—Lord Combermere was a guest at Eldridge's Plantation, next to Christ Church. At noon he sat on the verandah with his host, Mr R. Bowcher Clarke—later Sir Robert—and several other guests. The talk centred on the inevitable subject: the vault.

Theories—scientific, psychic, and even facetious—were bandied about until some of the gentlemen grew heated. Suddenly the Governor slapped his thigh, jumped to his feet, and barked, 'We're becoming obsessed by this thing!—it's time we took a walk on the headland!'

Bowcher Clarke recruited eight unhappy Negroes from the fields and Combermere led the party to the churchyard. They found the Elliott vault outwardly no different than it had been on July 17th of the preceding year.

The rector of the parish, the Rev. Thomas Orderson, D.D., was sent for. There were now six of them—all men of honour and distinction, leaders of the community.

Beside the Governor stood Major the Hon. J. Finch, his military secretary and A.D.C. Close by were the Hon. Nathan Lucas, Mr Rowland Cotton, and the rich planter, Bowcher Clarke. The rector assured them that he had no objection to the vault being reopened.

Detailed accounts of what followed were written by three of the party—Combermere, Orderson, and Nathan Lucas. No strange happening has been more completely documented or better authenticated. If we reject such testimony, we might as well stop compiling history from contemporary documents!

Lucas tells us that a close inspection of the exterior showed not a stone had been touched.

'The cement was uncracked and the large impressions of the Governor's seal were as sharp and as perfect as on the day on which they were made.

'Each person present who, on the former occasion, had made his private mark, satisfied himself that it had not been tampered with.'

Combermere ordered the slab to be removed. The eight

Negroes hesitated, then edged forward. The cement was chipped away with some difficulty, then pressure was brought to bear on the marble. The slab could not be moved.

The Negroes grew very agitated, and had to be threatened with harsh penalties before they would renew the attempt. At last the great slab yielded an inch or two. The panting Negroes slowly edged it wider until it was possible to hold a lantern inside.

At once the party saw why the first attempt to move the stone had failed: resting against it on the inside was one of the massive, lead-encased coffins—upside down!

The investigators squeezed inside, Combermere holding the lantern high. All was in bewildering confusion—all, that is, except the flimsy, loosely tied remains of Mrs Goddard's wooden coffin, which stood exactly as it had been left against the rear wall.

Standing on the bottom step with the others behind him the Governor lowered the lantern to inspect the floor. The layer of fine white sand lay everywhere, undisturbed by the slightest mark.

It was more than enough. The Governor emerged pale and silent. A few hours later he signed an order for the vault to be closed and the dead buried elsewhere in the churchyard. Seldom was an order carried out with such alacrity. . . .

Of the reopening, Lucas writes: 'I examined the walls, the arch, and every part of the vault, and found every part old and similar; and a mason in my presence struck every part with a hammer, and all was solid. I confess myself at a loss to account for the movement of these leaden coffins. Thieves certainly had no hand in it; and as for practical wit or hoax, too many were requisite to be trusted with the secret for it to remain unknown; and as for the Negroes having anything to do with it, their superstitious fear of the dead and everything belonging to them preclude any idea of this kind.

'All I know is that it happened, that I was an eye-witness of the fact!'

The Rev. Orderson, in a signed memorandum which Lucas appended to his manuscript, rejected other theories.

'Now how could one of the leaden coffins be set upon end against the wall?' he asks. '. . . Why was the bundle of Mrs Goddard's decayed coffin found where it had been left? Wood certainly would float first.

'There was no vestige of water to be discovered in the vault; no marks where it had been; and the vault is in a level churchyard, by no means in a fall, much less in a run of water.

'Earthquake could not have done this without levelling the churchyard to the ground.'

Nor is any feasible, non-mystic explanation offered in the many other versions—the *Memoirs and Correspondence of Field-Marshal Viscount Combermere*; Schomburgh's *History of Barbados*; Sir J. E. Alexander's *Transatlantic Sketches*; Sir Algernon Aspinall's essay *A Barbados Mystery*; Raymond Savage's *Barbados: British West Indies*, or Andrew Lang's later account, based on meticulous examination of all evidence available in manuscript form, which appeared in the *Folk-Lore Journal* for December 1907.

Numerous sketches and scale drawings of the Elliott vaults are available. It is a small one—twelve feet long by six feet six inches wide in floor space. It is partly above ground, partly below, and the sides slope inwards towards the top. Today the upper portion's large blocks of coral are cemented as firmly together as ever they were.

From inside the roof appears arched; seen from the outside it is perfectly flat. Beneath the dust and rubbish, the limestone floor is smooth and without a crevice.

Yet, even in this enlightened age, few care to venture near that end of the churchyard at night. For where no natural explanation can be found, men's thoughts turn to the *super*natural. . . .

What forces worked in the dark stillness of the sealed tomb? The hundred and fifty-year-old question remains unanswered, a tantalising challenge from the past to the science of today.

As you wrestle with the problem, searching for a solution in terms of the *known* and *proved*, you may deem it wise to forget this last sinister fact:

Three of the six coffins in the Elliott vault held the remains of people who had met violent deaths: both Thomas and Dorcas Chase were suicides, and Samuel Brewster was murdered by mutinous slaves.
Unsolved Mysteries, by Valentine Dyall.

But is this one of the world's great unsolved mysteries? Valentine Dyall offers a more natural explanation:

GIANT FUNGI?

'When this story was first published in *Everybody's Weekly*, on July 19th 1952, Mr Gregory Ames, of 50 Bonser Road, Twickenham, Middlesex, sent me a copy of a letter written by his great-grandfather on Christmas Day 1820.

'My dear Mother,

'I write regarding the interment of our infant relative, Samuel Brewster Ames. My own account of the opening of the tomb, as you will see, agrees substantially with the reports of the three witnesses. Before requesting Mr Clarke to reopen the tomb, however, I made some private examination.

'An aged Negro avers that mysterious explosive sounds in the sealed and empty tomb conduced to the remains of the Hon. John Elliott being buried elsewhere in 1724.

'We know that the force responsible for the "happening" is one capable of lifting great weights and yet subject to some geographical limitations: for not all the remains were disturbed. Vegetative growth of a fungoid character fulfils all these requirements. The explanation, therefore, is physical.

'Men of science have recorded that giant spherical fungi, similar to our native puffball, but having a circumference of over twenty feet, grow in caverns in Honduras. Though anchored in crevices by a threadlike stem, these fungi will lift great rocks. When ripe the spheres explode noisily, disintegrating into fine powder. Favourable winds could carry the spore to Barbados.

'I beseech you, therefore, mother, to have no fear that little Samuel's soul is in torment, but rather to consider kindly that his remains have been the means of making manifest yet one more wonder of Nature.'   *Unsolved Mysteries*, by Valentine Dyall.

Does Mr Ames's great-grandfather's explanation solve the mystery of *The Unquiet Tomb*?

There are many examples from nature of how the seemingly weak and fragile can perform quite astonishing feats of strength and endurance: how the tiny ant can move objects many times its own weight, or how a slender blade of grass can force its way through a concrete path. Can you think of other examples?

Or could the disturbances have been caused by a poltergeist like one of those described earlier in the chapter?

Or was it the supernatural power of voodoo, the native witchcraft that moved the coffins? In the next chapter you will read something of the uncanny power of the native witchdoctor. Could a relative of one of those buried in the vault have offended a voodoo priest who used his powers to desecrate the tomb and thus exact his revenge? Discuss your theories.

There are certain human beings who possess unusual traits that defy analysis and set them apart from the rest of humanity.

One such person was Hsieh Hsuan, a sixteenth-century Chinaman who was born with transparent flesh. Throughout his life his bones and internal organs could plainly be seen.*

* *Believe It or Not*, by Robert L. Ripley.

Samadhi, or suspended animation, the ability to slow down all bodily functions to the point of hibernation is a goal anxiously sought after by certain Indian yogi. One of the most amazing examples of this feat was performed in Lahore in 1837, by Haridas, a Hindu yogi.* Haridas went into a trance and helpers sealed up his ears, nose, eyes, and mouth with wax, bound him in a cloth and placed him in a grave which was then packed tight with earth. Guards were placed on duty night and day to make sure no deception took place. Forty days later, the grave was reopened and Haridas, emaciated but none the worse for his ordeal, climbed out.

A young American Negro, A. W. Underwood, defied medical science with his 'dragon breath'. He could set fire to leaves and pieces of cloth in a matter of seconds by pressing them close to his mouth and breathing through them. He allowed doctors to rinse his mouth out with various chemicals and wore rubber gloves to prevent any chance of fraud, but these precautions had no effect upon his strange powers.†

Perhaps there is some connection between Underwood's ability to set fire to materials and the tragic cases of those to whom internal combustion has meant a fiery death. Eric Frank Russell describes some of those who have suffered the terrifying agony of an . . .

ORDEAL BY FIRE

Every once in a while somebody bursts into flames in circumstances devoid of any obvious reason. Authority then finds itself stuck with a mystery, fiddles around with it and gets nowhere. More often than not the affair terminates when a baffled coroner's jury pronounces an issue-dodging verdict of 'accidental death'. A day, a week, or a month later another one roasts to death and the case goes through the same process.

There is plenty of evidence to suggest that in certain highly complicated and fortunately not too common conditions a human being can burst into flames or, in much rarer instances, flare up with near-explosive force. It does not happen often, but there is little doubt that it really does occur from time to time. In all my personal collection of data, extending over twenty-five years, I have found only one instance in which experts admitted the possibility of death by what may be called spontaneous combustion.

On December 28 1938, the *Sheffield Star* reported a Mrs Amelia Ridge burned to death for no reason whatsoever. Nothing could have caused it. The *Daily Telegraph*, of the same date, published a small list of equally mysterious self-cremations: Sarah Pegler at Aston Street, Birmingham; Ellen Wright at Melbourne Street,

* *Believe It or Not*, by Robert L. Ripley.
† *Strange People*, by Frank Edwards.

Carlisle; Harriet Lawless at Battersby Lane, Warrington; Harriet Garner at Lind Street, Walton, Liverpool.

Since distance destroys the news value of such personal tragedies, none of these papers reported any similar instances on the same date in other parts of the world. They gave five; the true total might have been fifty or five hundred. In the last one cited above, that of Harriet Garner, her son, Joseph Garner, deposed at the inquest that he had found his mother lying amid flaming bedclothes with no fire or light in the room, nothing to account for the blaze. Before she died she had been 'totally unable to explain what had happened'.

Mrs Selina Broadhursts, Wrexham, North Wales, was burned to a crisp by her own clothes in circumstances where it was not possible—*Liverpool Echo*, January 2nd 1939. Mrs Sarah Butcher was incinerated in a blaze that also devoured her son, Fred, according to *Reynolds News*, November 6th 1938. Would-be rescuers were driven back by the fury of the flames. The same paper reported one week earlier a similar tragedy in Elswick Road, Newcastle-upon-Tyne.

On December 27th 1938, the *Daily Telegraph* and several other papers reported Mrs Florence Hill of Croydon, Mrs Agnes Flight of Brixton, and Mrs Louisa Gorringe of Downham, Kent, all inexplicably burned to death. James Duncan of Ballina, Co. Mayo, Ireland, became a pillar of flaming agony in his own bedroom. 'So fierce the fire . . . that rescuers were unable to approach.'

Most of the victims were old, some bedridden, but none smoked large cigars in bed and scattered hot ash around. They weren't even near a light. The press described all these cases as 'mysteries'. Data of this kind can be found back to the year dot or forward to this morning. Selections given here are taken mostly from one comparatively short pre-war period to show the frequency of them.

Liverpool Echo, January 7th 1939—Mrs N. Edwards, Makin Street, Walton, Liverpool, was burned to death by her own clothes which caught fire, nobody knows how. 'There was no fire or light in the house at the time.' *Reynolds News*, June 12th 1948 —A woman at Butterworth was burned to death when her clothes 'inexplicably' caught fire. *Liverpool Echo*, July 30th 1938—A woman was burned to death on a cruiser on the Norfolk Broads. A policeman said, 'Apparently her clothes caught fire', but it beat him completely how they did it.

On September 20th 1938, the *Daily Telegraph* published the story of a woman who burst into flames bang in the middle of a dance-hall. She had not been smoking. Nobody bearing a cigarette had gone near her. There was not a fire or a naked light in the place. Couples glided about the floor, others chatted and sipped soft drinks. In the middle of the floor a shrill, tearing scream and a bellow of flames. She roared like a blow-torch and no man could save her. At the inquest Coroner L. F. Beccles listened to the evidence of many dumbfounded witnesses, then said, 'From all my experience I have never come across a case as mysterious as this!'

A violent fire of completely unknown origin killed Peter Seaton, aged eleven months, at Peckham Rye, London—*Daily Telegraph*, January 4th 1939. Superintendent E. H. Davies, of London's fire department, said the blaze began in the child's room but 'there was nothing whatever to suggest that it originated near an electric fire there'. A witness, Harold Edwin Huxstep, who vainly tried to rescue the child, said, 'It seemed as if I had opened a furnace door. There was a mass of flame and I was flung back across the hall. My hair caught alight and it was impossible to get Peter out.' Apparently, Peter Seaton and his bed flared up for the hell of it. Verdict: Accidental death.

Horace Trew Nicholas may have been an extraordinarily violent burner or else the victim of something never identified. There is no way of telling. At any rate, there was a bang in Windmill Road, Hampton Hill, London, and Horace Trew Nicholas went up like a rocket. He landed against the chimney stack on the roof of an adjacent house, clothes ablaze, hair burned off, rubber boots melted on his feet.—*Daily Telegraph*, December 28th 1939.

Experts said the cause was a coal-gas explosion. The gas company's experts rushed along, tore up the street in search of a gas-pocket or a leak, and found none. The first guessers then switched to sewer-gas. The municipal experts dashed in, mauled the street a second time, discovered no evidence of it. The coroner's jury then called it accidental death and left it at that.

If anything can create a spectacular bonfire it is a car with its highly inflammable upholstery and rubber tyres, engine full of oil and smeared with it from bumper to bumper, petrol tank loaded with liquid explosive. A peculiarity of human burnings is the way in which fires confine themselves to the victim despite combustible temptations all around, and this holds good even when the said victim is in a car. People have been burned swiftly and ferociously inside cars that suffered amazingly little damage, the resulting set-up pointing to a blaze of decidedly abnormal character.

A datum mailed in 1941, not marked with source but quoted from a Dutch newspaper, says that in 1938 a Netherlander was lugged from his car near Nimegen, Holland. His car was little damaged, its doors opened easily, its petrol tank was intact. The body was a cinder.

The *Sheffield Independent*, April 8th 1938, reported a case substantially the same. G. A. Shepherdson, a Hull building contractor, drove past a new housing project near Hessle, Yorkshire. He waved cheerily to friends as he went by and suffered superfast cremation one minute later.

He was burned to death 'with startling suddenness'. Experts confessed themselves completely puzzled, which refreshing honesty does something to restore one's faith in them. Police gave evidence that the petrol tank of Shepherdson's car was found full and undamaged, the car's doors opened easily, but inside lay that carbonised body charred by God alone knows what.

By some sort of coincidence the same thing happened in almost the same place ten years later. In early 1949 the *Sheffield Star* reported that the body of an unknown man had been dragged from his undamaged car near Hessle, Yorkshire. 'It was too badly burned to identify.' Doors opened without the faintest trouble, the petrol tank was intact, there was nothing to show how or why the occupant had been fried.

A Birkenhead truck-driver became a human firework at Upton-by-Chester—*Liverpool Echo*, April 7th 1938. He was incinerated in the cab of his vehicle in no time at all. At the inquest police witnesses said that they had found the petrol tank full and unharmed by fire, the doors of the cab opened easily, but the interior was 'a veritable furnace'. The coroner's jury stewed it over, wagged their heads, said 'accidental death', and added that there was nothing to show how the accident had occurred.

An especially valuable datum has disappeared, perhaps having burst into flames the moment my back was turned. I am forced to draw from memory. It was culled from a true crime story magazine in the early 1950s.

According to this, the Florida State Police devoted a good deal of time, patience, and intelligence to trying to solve a murder that was not a murder. They had found the burned corpse of an elderly lady in the sitting room of her large house where she lived alone. Neighbours had become alarmed at her absence and called the police.

The body reposed in a chair the cushions of which were slightly charred. The chair itself was scorched, also a circular patch of floor beneath. Combustion has been so fierce that fat roasted from the body had dripped down between the floorboards. The corpse was in such a state that identification could be made only by examination of bones, dental work, metal buttons, jewellery, and other items that had survived the blaze.

The room was stacked with enough stuff to cause a major fire but for some mysterious reason it had not caught. Flames had confined themselves to the body, the chair and the floor immediately beneath. On the face of it, the victim had been murdered. Somebody had then poured volatile liquid over the corpse and set fire to it in an effort to conceal the crime.

Police set to work on this theory. The corpse, or what there was of it, was shipped to a laboratory for scientific examination. Fire specialists practically took the death-room apart. Uniformed police and plain-clothes detectives raked the neighbourhood for information on visitors, lurkers, suspicious characters, or any other lead.

The victim's personal background was dug out and analysed for evidence of anyone bearing her a grudge. Known mental cases, ex-convicts, drug-addicts, house-breakers, and pyro-maniacs for miles around were picked up, and taken in for questioning and put through the mill. Relatives, friends, and acquaintances of the victim were cross-examined repeatedly. Anyone remotely likely to benefit from the death had a rough time, with every minute of their alibis checked and rechecked.

After many weeks of intensive work the result was complete stalemate. It was now known that nobody had visited the house around the time of the fatality, nobody had broken into it by force, and nothing of value was missing. The victim's charred skeleton bore no evidence of violence; analysis of the ashes showed that she had not been doused with inflammable fluid. Nobody had fallen out with her, had any reason to envy or hate her. All her beneficiaries were in the clear, in fact the most logical suspects had been hundreds of miles away at the time of death and were able to prove it.

A long, frustrating list of negatives saying it had happened and that was all. Not satisfied, the baffled police chief sent complete details of the case to several authorities specialising in fire fatalities, and finally received from one source the assurance that death can be caused by spontaneous combustion and that, although not very common, other similar cases were on record. This is the only instance where the fact has been admitted.

The genius who can always be trusted not to pass up a single extraordinary phenomenon, namely Charles Fort, added such items to his collection a quarter of a century ago. The two following are taken from *The Books of Charles Fort*.

The *Daily News*, December 17th 1904—Mrs Thomas Cochrane, Rosehill, Falkirk, Scotland, was found dead in her chair 'surrounded by pillows and cushions'. There was no fire in the grate, no candle, lamp, or any other light in the room. The pillows and cushions were not so much as scorched. But she was 'burned almost beyond recognition'.

On December 27th and 28th 1916, *New York Herald* reported that Lillian Green, a housekeeper at the Lake Denmark Hotel, seven miles from Dover, New Jersey, had been found badly burned and dying. Her clothes and the floor beneath her were charred but nothing else in the room showed the slightest trace of fire or possible origin of fire. At the hospital the victim was able to speak but totally unable to explain what happened. She died without explaining.

Even in this very small selection from a frighteningly massive whole we have two cases far apart in time and space but remarkably alike in their finale. Harriet Garner in Liverpool in 1938, and Lillian Green in New Jersey in 1916, both survived long enough to talk. The result is described in identical words: 'they were totally unable to explain what had happened'. Obviously neither knew what happened. They had burst into flames pathetically believing it impossible for people to burst into flames and even after the event neither could accept that what cannot happen had happened. It can and does happen.

A broad survey of such cases shows that almost anyone can burst into flames at any time or place, regardless of age or sex. But analysis of the same survey demonstrates a great preponderance of cases in given conditions. A huge majority occurs indoors, to elderly people, especially those of the female sex. Victimisation of females may be no more than a misleading statistic; in most countries women outnumber men, live longer than men, and at any given time there are far more old ladies than old men ambling around.

It looks very much as though a considerable fire hazard is suffered by those old enough or sufficiently tramplike in habits to be overclothed and somewhat careless about matters of personal hygiene. Excessive warmth, some dampness caused by perspiration or urine, the interaction of trace chemicals used to improve, bleach, dye, and preshrink fabrics, plus friction caused by normal movement, all these combine once in a while to set up a blaze for which the body itself is also ready and burns furiously along with the clothes.

When thirteen years old and a member of a secret gang of juvenile delinquents I took part in certain nefarious activities not the least of which was the manufacture of explosives in our abandoned henhouse headquarters. This sinister research terminated when we blew off the roof and tattooed two members for life with the aid of an ill-judged and over-generous dollop of gunpowder.

One of our favourite concoctions was brewed with ammonia and iodine. We mixed the stuff, filtered it through a newspaper and dried the residue. The result was a brownish powder so incredibly sensitive that it could be exploded by the impact of a fly alighting upon it. For quite a time no man was safe, police especially. One unwary step in the night would be greeted with a crack, a flash, and a puff of purple smoke.

The human system contains iodine, daily expels a certain amount of it. Urine is exceedingly rich in ammonia. Couple these facts with carelessness in matters of hygiene and you have a set-up which I do not for one moment offer as the true or likely cause of human burnings but which serves to show what can happen.

Great World Mysteries, by Frank Russell.

Why do certain people burst into flames? I expect you have all heard of cases where people have been smoking even though explicitly forbidden to do so, either for reasons of health or because the nature of their work brings them into contact with highly inflammable materials, and, to avoid being caught, have pocketed a cigarette or pipe, not properly extinguished, and thereby set their clothes on fire.

Or you may have heard of others who have died because they did not follow the maker's instructions to have their electric blankets checked regularly.

How many of the cases quoted in the article could come in these two categories?

We all know how articles of clothing made from nylon can sparkle in the dark when taken off. In 1955 the *Daily Express* reported a case in Stockholm where a spark produced by the friction of a female worker's nylon underwear caused an explosion in an ammunition factory.

Have you heard of any recent cases of people bursting into flames for no apparent reason?

The sea has always held a fascination for man. Sailors are extremely superstitious by nature and many are the legends and mysteries connected with the deep. The *Flying Dutchman*, destined until doomsday to battle around the stormy Cape; the strange disappearance of three keepers from the lighthouse on Eilean Mor;

the mysterious sea monster, an enormous serpent, like some pre-historic survival, recorded in many a ship's log.

Stories concerning ships lost at sea are legion. The very vastness of the ocean, covering as it does five-sevenths of the earth's surface, hinders the search.

In 1908, in the days before air-sea rescue, the 16,000 ton British owned passenger and cargo liner, the *Waratah*, was the very latest thing in ship's design. On July 25th 1909 she left Durban for Cape-town on the homeward run from Australia with over one hundred passengers and crew and ten thousand tons of cargo. On the after-noon of July 27th a tremendous storm sprang up in the Indian Ocean which lasted for thirty-six hours. It was during this storm that the *Waratah* vanished completely.

In spite of an extensive search not a trace of the large liner was to be found. Perhaps, with steering gear broken and her powerful engines put out of action by the raging hurricane, she drifted way off course to become trapped in an Antarctic ice pack or holed by an iceberg. At the court of inquiry various experts pronounced her unsafe. Perhaps, unable to breast the raging seas she heeled over and plunged to the bottom. No one really knows.*

Ship's crews too have vanished, lost without trace. In 1880 the inhabitants of the fishing village of Easton's Beach near Newport, Rhode Island, were amazed to see a ship in full sail bearing down upon them, finally going aground upon the sandy beach. She was the *Seabird* returning to Newport from Honduras. The only passenger on board was a mongrel dog belonging to one of the crew. Coffee was boiling on the stove and the table in the galley was laid for breakfast, but there was no solution to the mystery of why the crew should have disappeared from their ship so near to their homes.†

The most famous case of a disappearing crew is undoubtedly that of the *Mary Celeste*.

THE MYSTERY OF THE *MARY CELESTE*

At three o'clock, or thereabouts, on the afternoon of December 5th 1872, the *Dei Gratia*, a brig of Nova Scotia, bound from New York to Gibraltar under the command of Captain Morehouse, was about three hundred and eighty miles from the coast of Portugal. Her position was officially reported as latitude 38 degrees 20 minutes North and longitude 17 degrees 15 minutes West. She was on a course a little to the north of the direct route, being about midway between the Azores and Cape Roca on the Portuguese coast, some three hundred and seventy miles from the island of Santa Maria.

* *Unsolved Mysteries*, by Valentine Dyall.
† *Strangely Enough*, by C. B. Colby.

The sea was calm and there was a light wind from the north. There were, it is said, two other vessels within sight of the *Dei Gratia*. One of these was a German tramp steamer outward bound for the West Indies. Later, when she reached port and heard talk of a derelict found in rather queer circumstances, the tramp's crew said that they remembered sighting, on the day and in the latitude mentioned, a strange brig about three miles to starboard. They had signalled to her, and been a little puzzled to get no reply. This had argued a want of sea manners, but the distance between the two ships was too great, and the matter too trivial, to engage further attention.

It must have been a little later in the afternoon that the *Dei Gratia*, sailing on the port tack, began to overhaul this same strange brig, which had all her sails set and was on the port tack, her headsails, however (jib and foretopmast staysail), being set to starboard. As the *Dei Gratia* came up with her, Captain Morehouse, to his surprise, recognised her as the *Mary Celeste*, which had been loading her cargo in New York at the same time as the *Dei Gratia*, but had put to sea a few days earlier. He and Briggs, the Master of the *Mary Celeste*, were old friends, and had actually dined together in New York on the night before the *Mary Celeste* sailed. It was therefore only natural that Morehouse should signal to the other ship, but by no means so natural that the *Mary Celeste* should keep on, as she did, without giving any reply. As the interval between the two ships lessened, Morehouse was still more puzzled by the haphazard sailing of the *Mary Celeste*; for instead of making a steady course, she was yawing and, when the wind shifted a point, running off aimlessly before it. Another circumstance struck him as strange: whereas both ships were sailing on the port tack, the jib and foretopmast staysail of the *Mary Celeste* were set on the starboard tack. Obviously something was amiss, and when Morehouse called his mate to have a look at the other ship and asked him what he thought was the matter, the mate made the obvious answer that it looked as though the crew were below drunk.

By this time the ships were about half a mile from each other. Still no answer came from the *Mary Celeste*, nor, scan her decks as they might, could the men in the *Dei Gratia* detect a sign of life aboard. They gave her an urgent hoist and, a few moments later, as the two ships drove yet closer, Morehouse hailed the brig. When the decks remained silent and empty, he began to feel alarmed. He ordered a boat to be lowered and manned by the first mate, Oliver Deveau, and a couple of men.

As the boat neared the brig, the three men could see the name, plainly painted upon her stern—*Mary Celeste*, New York. That ended any doubt of her identity; and, so far as they could see as they came alongside, there was nothing wrong. Here was no waterlogged derelict, but a sound craft, her sails set, her timbers undamaged, and yet apparently not a soul aboard her. What was the explanation—mutiny, or piracy, or what?

Coming alongside, the mate ordered one of the men to stay in the boat, while he and the other clambered up by the chain plates and hoisted themselves aboard. On deck they could see no one and hear nothing but the thud of their own footsteps, the creaking of the blocks, and the occasional slap of a sail. No one was at the wheel; the brig, it seemed, was sailing herself, unless, like the Phantom Ship of the old story, she was manned by a supernatural crew. Completely mystified, and possibly a little alarmed, the mate signalled to Captain Morehouse to join him.

With the arrival of the Master a careful examination of the ship began. Cautiously the two men walked aft, looking keenly about them; then forward again; and then below deck. They searched the ship from stem to stern, finding no one and detecting no sign of trouble. At last they came to a standstill, baffled. Here was a ship undoubtedly derelict, and yet, so far as they could observe, perfectly sound. Her hull, masts, and yards were in good condition; her cargo, which consisted of a number of barrels of alcohol, was properly stowed and in order; and there was no lack of food or water. On deck, it is true, one small point drew their attention. A hatch had been displaced and lay, wrong side up, close to the hatchway it had covered. That was not much of a clue.

Almost as puzzling as the absence of any living person aboard was the lack of any trace, not only of a reason for abandoning the ship, but of the actual process of evacuation. At least one would have expected to find marks of disorder or confusion; but there was nothing. It was as though the men of the *Mary Celeste* had been pursuing their usual routine when by some strange agency they had been spirited away.

In the forecastle, for example, the seamen's chests were untouched; some razors lying about were bright and unrusted, and garments were hanging out to dry on a line; while among the dunnage were an English note for five pounds and other articles which were, one might have supposed, sufficiently valuable to be taken by their owners on leaving the ship.

In the galley everything was in order, just as the cook would have left it after he had cleared away the aftermath of a meal.

The cabin, again, yielded nothing in the way of a clue. There was a melodeon or harmonium, its cover was raised as though it had been in recent use, and on a rack near by was an open sheet of music; on the table was a sewing-machine with a piece of cloth that might have been a child's pinafore fixed in it; and a small oilcan, a thimble, and a reel of cotton, all of them objects easily displaced by the motion of the ship, lay beside it. On the same table was a slate containing some notes for the log and showing November 25th as the date of the last entry; and there was an unfinished letter, apparently from the mate of the *Mary Celeste*, beginning, 'Fanny, my dear wife'. The writer had got so far when something interrupted him. There were books and music, mostly of a religious character, undisturbed and unharmed, and spare panes of glass were found stowed away and unbroken. The Captain's watch was hanging from the lamp-bracket over the table. According to some accounts, the accuracy of which I cannot guarantee, there were also the remains of a half-eaten breakfast in the cabin, a plate with a little porridge on it and an egg with the top sliced off. The general inference to be drawn from the state of the cabin was that, whatever had been the nature of the calamity which had turned the *Mary Celeste* into a derelict, it was not stress of weather.

Some further discoveries were made in the Captain's cabin. Trinkets of some small value, and including at least one gold locket, had been left behind, and in one of the bunks, which looked as though it had been occupied by a child, the imprint of a head was still clearly visible on the pillow. As the other berths in the cabin had all been made up, it seemed reasonable to conclude that the ship must have been abandoned in the late morning or afternoon, a conclusion which perhaps goes against the story of the breakfast débris.

Clearly the crew had been in a hurry and had had time to take very little with them. A drawer in the storeroom seemed to have been hastily emptied of some tins of preserved meat; the ship's papers, with the exception of the log-book, were missing; and there was no sign of the Captain's chronometer. The ship's boat had gone, and the davits were swung out with trailing ropes.

Captain Morehouse next turned to the log. The last day's work recorded was on November 24th, eleven days earlier, when an observation taken placed the vessel in latitude 36 degrees 56 Minutes North and longitude 27 degrees 20 minutes West; in other words, about a hundred and ten miles west of the island of Santa Maria in the Azores. Entries on the slate, however, had been carried on up to eight o'clock on the following morning, when apparently the ship was passing north of the island, the eastern point of which, at the time of the entry, bore S.S.W. at a distance of six miles. That was the last record of any kind, and the problem, as it appeared at once to Morehouse, is what could have happened after eight o'clock on the morning of November 25th and how the *Mary Celeste*, unmanned and unsteered, held on her course for the better part of ten days and nights, until she reached the point, some three hundred and seventy-three miles east of the island of Santa Maria, where the *Dei Gratia* found her.

That she should have sailed so far and for so long on the port tack with her jib and foretopmast staysail set on the starboard tack is not so improbable as it may sound. The prevailing wind was north during those eleven days, and with the sails set as they were the course might well have been at about a right angle to the direction of the wind. When she came to the wind, the jibs would back her off; and if she fell away, the mainsail would drive her into the wind again.

The men from the *Dei Gratia*, baffled as they were, did make two further discoveries, which were thought of possible significance. The first of these was a cutlass which, when taken out of its scabbard, showed signs of having been smeared with blood and afterwards wiped. The idea of foul play, which this at once suggested, was supported by the detection of what looked like spots of blood on the deck, close to the displaced hatch. Yet more stains, which might have been blood, were observed on the starboard topgallant rail, and close to them a deep cut, such as a sharp axe might have made, was detected. The other discovery seemed quite without meaning. On either side of the bows of the ship, some two or three feet above the water-line, a narrow strip had been cut away from the edge of one of the outer planks, to a depth of about three-eighths of an inch, a width of about one and a quarter inches, and a length of between six and seven feet. The injury was recent, obviously intentional, and apparently caused by a sharp cutting instrument.

With these unsatisfying results the search for the moment ended. Captain Morehouse could make nothing of the business, but salvage was salvage, and a windfall that does not drop on every day of the week. So the mate and two men being left aboard to work the derelict, the two ships continued their interrupted voyage to Gibraltar.

Since not only the mystery of the *Mary Celeste*, but her very existence, have been disputed, the contemporary evidence is important. No fewer than six separate numbers of *Lloyd's List* in 1872 and 1873 mention her and her misadventure; while *The Times* of December 30th 1873, carries a short paragraph giving the story of her discovery and arrival in Gibraltar. In the *American Record of Shipping* she appears as a half-brig or brigantine of 282 tons, built in 1861 at Parrsborough in Novia Scotia. She was therefore a two masted ship with square sails on her foremast and fore and aft sails on her mainmast. Her length was ninety-eight feet, her beam was twenty-five feet, and her draught eleven feet two inches.

In 1872 her principal owner was Captain J. H. Winchester, of J. H. Winchester & Company, New York, but three men, one of whom was Captain Briggs himself, held shares in the ship, and a certain Mr Hart had a mortgage on it.

From the *Maritime Register* we learn that the *Mary Celeste* sailed from New York for Genoa on November 7th 1872, under the command of Captain Benjamin S. Briggs, of Marion, Massachusetts. As some of the so-called explanations of the mystery which were to appear show him in a most unfavourable light, it should be made clear that, from all the evidence, he bore the highest character, both at his home in New England, where he and his family were well known and much respected, and in Gibraltar, where his frequent calls had made him a familiar figure. He was a man of about forty-five, ruddy and whiskered, and was described by those who knew him best as a typical sailing-master of the old school. He was a bit of a disciplinarian, a strict teetotaller, and, weather permitting, made it his daily practice, when at sea, to read a chapter of the Bible.

On this last voyage he was accompanied by his wife Sarah, who had sailed with him before, and by their little daughter, aged two, from whom, as she was little more than a baby, her mother did not wish to be separated. Besides the Briggs family, the *Mary Celeste* carried seven men. The first mate was Albert G. Richardson, of Maine; the second mate was Andrew Gilling of New York; the steward and cook was Edward William Head, of New York. The rest of the company were Volkerk Lorenzen, Bos Lorenzen, Arian Harbens, and Gottlieb Goodshaad. There were in all, therefore, ten people on board. In most of the stories which later appeared, ample licence was taken both as to the names and the number of the crew. Naturally the favourite number is thirteen, but the names vary widely and picturesquely.

The *Mary Celeste* carried a cargo of seventeen hundred barrels of alcohol, consigned to Messrs H. Mascarenhas & Co. of Genoa, for use in fortifying Italian wines.

So much is plain, verifiable fact.

The arrival of the *Dei Gratia* with a derelict and a strange story created a considerable stir at Gibraltar, particularly as Captain Briggs was no stranger on the Rock. What could have happened to him and his crew? Morehouse of course had no answer. He could only tell his story and put in his claim for salvage. But before any award could be made, an inquiry had to be held, and the result of this was reported to the British Board of Trade by Mr Solly Flood, "Her Majesty's Advocate-General and Proctor for the Queen in her Office of Admiralty, and Attorney-General for Gibraltar."

Mr Flood began by giving the story of the finding of the ship, of her arrival in Gibraltar, and of the claim to salvage put in by the Master of the *Dei Gratia*. He and the mate were examined and 'the account which they gave of the soundness and good condition of the derelict was so extraordinary that I found it necessary to apply for a survey.' This was carried out by Mr Ricardo Portunato, a diver, Mr John Austin, Master Surveyor of Shipping, and a Mr T. J. Vecchio. 'From that survey it appears that both bows of the derelict had been recently cut by a sharp instrument, but that she was thoroughly sound, staunch, strong, and in every way seaworthy and well found; that she was well provisioned, and that she had encountered no seriously heavy weather; and that no appearance of fire or explosion, or of alarm of fire or explosion, or any other assignable cause for abandonment, was discoverable. A sword, however, was found, which appeared to me to exhibit traces of blood, and to have been wiped before being returned into its scabbard.' Thoroughly puzzled, Mr Flood then made a second examination, in which he was assisted by four naval officers and a Colonel in the Royal Engineers. They all agreed that the injury to the bows was intentional and not accidental. They discovered the stains and the cut on the starboard topgallant rail. They further found that a barrel of alcohol under the forehatch had been tampered with. After describing the contents of the Captain's cabin, of the ship's log, and of the slate log, Mr Flood gave his own conclusion. 'My own theory or guess is that the crew got at the alcohol and in the fury of drunkenness murdered the Master, whose name was Briggs, his wife and child, and the chief mate; that they then damaged the bows of the vessel, with the view of giving it the appearance of having struck on rocks or suffered a collision, so as to induce the Master of any vessel which might pick them up, if they saw her at some distance, to think her not worth attempting to save; and that they did, some time between November 25th and December 5th, escape on board some vessel bound for some

North or South American port or the West Indies.' In support of his report Mr Flood appended affidavits from Austin, Surveyor of Shipping at Gibraltar, and Portunato the diver.

To all this must be added the independent evidence of Captain Shufeldt, of the American ship *Plymouth*, then in Gibraltar, whose conclusions were published in the *Gibraltar Chronicle* of March 4th 1873. He thought that the *Mary Celeste* might have been 'strained in a gale and for the time leaked so much as seriously to alarm the Master, and it is possible that at this time another vessel in sight induced him, as his wife and child were on board, to abandon his ship thus hastily.' Shufeldt altogether rejected the idea of a mutiny and thought the injury to the bows was merely caused by 'the action of the sea'. He maintained that 'the Master and crew will either be heard of some day or, if not, that they have perished in the boat for which they abandoned their own ship.' He adds one piece of information which Mr Flood omits. The alleged bloodstains on the cutlass and the rail had been analysed by a Dr Patron and found to be merely rust.

So we come to the verdict of the Vice-Admiralty Court, given on March 25th and reported in the *Gibraltar Chronicle* next day.

'In the Vice-Admiralty Court yesterday the Hon. the Chief Justice gave judgement in the *Mary Celeste* salvage case, and awarded the sum of £1700 to the Master and crew of the Nova Scotia brigantine *Dei Gratia* for the salvage services rendered by them; the cost of the suit to be paid out of the property salved. The *Mary Celeste* was valued at $5,700, and her cargo at $36,943, total $42,643, so that the award may be set down as one-fifth of the total value.'

The judgement ended on a note of censure. Captain Morehouse had allowed his first mate, Oliver Deveau, to obliterate some of the supposed stains of blood on the cutlass or the rail. As a result an analysis of the remaining stains had been necessary, and the judge ordered the cost of this to be charged against the amount awarded the salvors.

Two explanations of the mystery had come out. The official view, which the Treasury Department at Washington endorsed in its instructions to Customs Officers, was of mutiny and murder. To this there are some obvious objections. The evidence was of the slightest—bloodstains which turned out to be rust, an inexplicable injury to the bows, a cut on a rail, a displaced hatch, a broached barrel of alcohol. These hardly sustained the theory that three or four people had been done to death; and the orderly state of the ship went far to rebut it. Then there was the problem of what had become of the 'mutineers'. If they had boarded some passing vessel they would have had some difficulty in posing as distressed mariners. If they intended to tell a story of storm and shipwreck, surely they would have scuttled the *Mary Celeste*; for a more awkward piece of evidence than that floating conundrum can scarcely be imagined. But they would have had to account for themselves somehow, and when they reached port, would have been marked men. The sea-ports of the world were on the look-out for them. A further point is the absence of any motive. Men do not mutiny for the fun of the thing; generally they are driven to it by their own greed or by the tyranny of their commander. But Briggs was a decent, respectable man with a good sea reputation, not at all the sort that would bully a crew into rebellion and murder. Nor was there anything in the ship of sufficient value to arouse cupidity. But if the motive was neither desperation nor greed, what was it? Finally, the theory of mutiny, although tenable for a few weeks after the arrival of the *Mary Celeste* at Gibraltar, was almost refuted by time. Not a single man of her company has ever turned up. Plenty of people have claimed to know, or to know of, men who sailed in her, and have come forward with some story to support their contention, but every one of these claims is demonstrably a fabrication.

The other opinion at Gibraltar was that of Captain Shufeldt, who rejected mutiny and believed the ship was abandoned in a panic. This was a likelier explanation than the other, though his suggestion that she might have sprung a leak in a gale is open to two objections. The first is that there was no gale, and the second that everyone who examined the *Mary Celeste* at Gibraltar agreed that she was in perfectly good condition without a trace of a leak. For some time hope persisted that some of the missing persons would turn up somewhere; but the weeks passed; nothing happened; and in the absence of any authentic explanation the legends began.

The various legends are not without interest. First in the field was Sir Arthur Conan Doyle with his 'J. Hababuk Jephson's Statement'. The name of the ship is misspelt *Marie Celeste*, and most of the details are imaginary, perhaps by design, as the tale hardly professes to be history, and after appearing in a magazine was included in a volume of short stories. Conan Doyle introduces a young accountant, a sinister quadroon,* and several black seamen into the ship's company. The coloured men, led by the quadroon, murdered all the whites except Jephson and were then taken off in boats by some African accomplices.

* A quadroon is a person of mixed race, one-quarter black, three-quarters white.

STRANGE UNSOLVED MYSTERIES

Conan Doyle had numerous imitators. They professed to be giving facts and, like him, added a second mystery to the first. Swallowing without question Doyle's assertion that the *Mary Celeste*, when found, was carrying her boat, their concern was as much to explain *how* as to explain *why* she was abandoned. All their attempts to produce authentic solutions are easily refuted. Some are fantastic; others are highly ingenious; and the liberties taken with the facts and the many unfounded reflections upon Briggs and Morehouse, when many of the relatives of both captains were still alive, are not easily defensible.

The fact is that the *Mary Celeste* should have carried two boats, a long-boat and a yawl. Unfortunately, while the cargo was being loaded at New York and the heavy barrels of alcohol were being swung aboard, a rope gave, and two of the kegs, slipping, fell on the long-boat and damaged it so badly that it was useless. Captain Briggs reported the mishap to his agents and asked for the boat to be replaced before he sailed; but for some reason or other this was not done, and the *Mary Celeste* put to sea carrying only her yawl, which, though able at a pinch to accomodate all her company, was of course smaller and less seaworthy than the long-boat. The presence aboard of the boat in any of these 'explanations' is enough by itself to stamp it as an invention.

Amid so much fiction, what was the truth? Why was the *Mary Celeste* abandoned? Morehouse, whose opinion is important, always believed that on the morning of November 25th the *Mary Celeste* was becalmed a few miles to the north of the rugged and precipitous coast of Santa Maria in the Azores; that a current began to drive her towards the shore; and that the crew in a fright took to the boat. Probably they intended to stand by and, if a breeze sprang up, rejoin their ship; but unfortunately they did not take the precaution of attaching the yawl by a line to the *Mary Celeste*. So, when the desired breeze came, the brigantine careered away from them and, row as strongly as they could, they were unable to overhaul her. Morehouse believed that ultimately the yawl was driven ashore and beaten to pieces in the surf at the foot of the cliffs, all in her perishing.

This was also the view of Captain James Briggs, a brother of the missing captain. Yet it is not altogether satisfactory. The last entry in the *Mary Celeste*'s log reported fine weather, a light wind, and land six miles distant. The ship might have been becalmed and drifted inshore a little later in the day, but the situation could hardly have called for so precipitate an evacuation as took place. Briggs was no raw youngster, but a sailor of experience, not the sort of man to abandon his ship save in extremity or, having ordered his men into a boat to await a favourable breeze, to omit the obvious precaution of hanging out a line, so that if a breeze came the ship could be regained.

For these reasons I prefer the solution of Brigg's cousin, Dr Oliver Cobb, who was a boy of fourteen in Massachusetts when the *Mary Celeste* sailed. He believed that the clue to the mystery is to be found in the cargo, which, it will be remembered, consisted of seventeen hundred barrels of alcohol. In normal circumstances, such a cargo, if properly stowed, should be quite safe, but experts in marine insurance have expressed the view that in certain conditions gases might be generated and danger ensue. Given a sufficiently high temperature, local explosions might occur and be followed possibly by a general explosion of the whole cargo. The result in a small ship like the *Mary Celeste* can be imagined. The seventeen hundred barrels of crude alcohol would blow her to pieces and destroy every soul on board.

This was also the theory of the principal owner, Captain J. H. Winchester, who crossed the Atlantic and was in Gibraltar in time to attend the salvage proceedings. As he was an experienced shipmaster, knew Briggs well, and had the opportunity of inspecting the ship while she was at Gibraltar, he was as qualified as anyone to give an opinion.

I would commend this explanation without hesitation were it not that the late Commander Rupert Gould, the well-known writer and broadcaster on odd occurrences, especially at sea, would have none of it, being unable to believe that a scare of fire and explosion would have left so little trace behind it. Besides, he had his own theory, which is much the same as was propounded by Oliver Deveau, the mate of the *Dei Gratia*. Gould and Deveau believed the ship had been abandoned in a panic, under the wrong impression that she was leaking badly. Since Briggs was an unlikely participant in either the faulty sounding of the well or the panic that followed, Gould concluded that he was no longer there. He was dead, perhaps from heart failure, perhaps swept overboard. So when the moment came, no one was there to act promptly and sensibly; the crew took to the boat, possibly without even food or water; and the *Mary Celeste*, still under sail, drew away. Subsequently the boat was either swamped or dashed to pieces on the shore of Santa Maria. Gould points out that something of the sort very nearly happened to Captain Cook's *Endeavour* in 1770, and may explain a much later puzzle, the arrival in 1919 of the schooner *Marion J. Douglas* off the Scillies, deserted, but still under sail, her crew having left her near the Newfoundland Banks under the impression that she was sinking.

There are, however, two objections to Gould's version. When the *Mary Celeste* was picked up, she showed no trace of leak or even of damage that might cause a leak. Captain Briggs is not known to have had a weak heart or his ship to have been in a gale; and if he had died, as Gould suggests, some entry to that effect would certainly have appeared in the log.

On the whole, therefore, and with due respect for Gould's dissent, I give my verdict to Captain Winchester, Dr Cobb, and the theory of a threatened explosion. Let us try to reconstruct the tragedy. On November 25th 1872, the *Mary Celeste* was a few miles from the island of Santa Maria. The weather was fine, a light wind was blowing, and we may assume that for the latitude and the time of year the day was pretty warm. As the *Mary Celeste* slipped along, pitching slightly in the Atlantic swell, we may suppose a danger signal. It may be that someone noticed a smell of gas lingering round the hatches; or possibly someone heard queer rumbling noises such as in a warm climate gas, escaping from alcohol, may make. The Captain ordered a hatch to be removed so that air might reach the cargo and disperse any gas that had formed. While the men were lifting the heavy hatch there was an explosion, overturning it and perhaps injuring one of the men working on it. There was alarm and possibly confusion, since at any moment a further explosion might blow the ship sky-high. Some of the men began to take in sail, others to lower the yawl. A moment later a second small explosion threw them into something like a panic. They did not stop to take in more sail or to lash the wheel. The Captain snatched up his chronometer and such of the ship's papers as he could quickly lay his hands on; someone burst open a drawer and took out a few tins of preserved meat; and all, without further delay, tumbled over the side into the yawl. Possibly, in the hurry of launching, the small, overcrowded boat capsized and all were drowned. Or perhaps they got clear of the ship. If so, their one thought would be to place as much water as possible between themselves and that perilous cargo, and they would row with desperate haste away from the *Mary Celeste*. But the minutes passed; nothing happened; they stopped rowing and watched. Presently the wind freshened and the brigantine ran away from them.

They may have tried to row after her and failed to reach her or, still haunted by the fear of an explosion, have turned the yawl's head towards the distant shore. They may have drawn near to the coast and been caught in the surf, the boat smashed and ten lives lost. No trace of it or them was even found, but the disappearance of a small boat in the Atlantic is a minor mystery.

Meanwhile the removal of the hatch had released the gases from the hold of the *Mary Celeste*, the fresh air had poured in and, all danger past, the brigantine sailed on unmanned.

This solution covers most of the facts. It explains the state of suspended routine, the headlong haste with which the ship was abandoned, the overturned hatch, the barrel of alcohol which bore signs of having been tampered with and doubtless was damaged in the explosion, possibly the spots of blood on the deck. The stains on the cutlass had been proved to be rust and the cuts on the bows had probably no connection with the affair.

The further history of the *Mary Celeste* deserves a note. After completing her voyage to Genoa, she returned to America. Here she was sold, and sold again and again. Sailors are superstitious and she had become a marked ship. No one much wanted to own her, or sail in her, or have anything to do with her. At the end of 1884 she made her last voyage. She ran aground on Roshell's Reef, off the coast of Haiti, and became a total loss. Subsequently her Master was indicted for barratry and conspiracy, the discovery having been made that her cargo, insured for about $30,000, was mostly rubbish. By a series of curious mischances almost everyone who had had anything to do with the voyage soon afterwards either died or came to grief. It was as though there was a curse on the *Mary Celeste*, to hold even when her timbers were rotting on Roshell's Reef.

The Mary Celeste and other strange tales of the Sea,
by J. G. Lockhart.

What do you think happened to the crew of the *Mary Celeste*? Do you agree with Solly Flood that they broke open a barrel of alcohol and, in a drunken frenzy, murdered the captain, his wife and child and later, when they had sobered up, damaged the bows of the ship to give the impression that she had been in a collision with another vessel or had hit a rock, and was therefore not worth salvaging: the assassins then boarding a passing ship to be taken to the safety of some foreign port?

Or do you believe Captain Morehouse's theory that, fearing the *Mary Celeste* was running aground, the crew took to the boat but forgot to attach it by line to the ship, finding, when the danger was past, that they could not catch up with her and were dashed to pieces on a rocky shore?

Or is Dr Oliver Cobb's theory more in keeping with the known facts? That a threatened explosion caused the crew to panic and take to the boat. Or, perhaps, Commander Rupert Gould's belief that the crew had mistakingly assumed the *Mary Celeste* to be leaking badly and had taken to the boat which later sank in the high seas?

Finally we have two further theories. Eric Frank Russell, in *Great World Mysteries*, believes that the bread eaten by the crew was made from flour containing ergot. This organism is highly poisonous and causes people who have eaten it to suffer terrible delusions, leading, in many cases, to suicide. Russell thinks that the crew, crazed by the effects of the drug, threw themselves overboard and were drowned.

Perhaps the strangest theory of all is that put forward by M. K. Jessup in his book *The Case for the U.F.O.* Jessup believed that the crew were kidnapped by the occupants of a flying saucer and were taken away to another planet.

Which of the above theories do you think the most convincing for the strange disappearance of the crew of the *Mary Celeste*? Or have you a better one?

JUNGLE WITCHCRAFT

Witchcraft is as old as mankind and even today, in spite of the great advances that have taken place in medical science, native witch-doctors are still found throughout the world. They practise their strange art in Africa, South America, Polynesia, Java, Malaya, Borneo, and Greenland. A witch-doctor must be a jack of all trades; hypnotist, psychologist, astrologer, weatherman, prophet, lawyer, conjurer, politician, showman, priest and doctor, living by his wits and the reputation that he builds up for himself within his own community. Training begins in childhood and only the strong in mind and body are able to survive the long and arduous ordeal imposed upon them by the elderly witch-doctors responsible for their tuition. They learn to protect their people by means of ointments and charms from evil spirits sent by enemy witch-doctors and with strange rites and invocations to ensure a plentiful harvest. They ferret out the lawbreakers and punish them unmercifully. Their methods of treating the sick are completely unorthodox by our own medical standards and yet they are remarkably effective as the following account illustrates.

In 1937 Harry B. Wright, an American dentist from Philadelphia, intrigued by stories of the remarkable cures performed by the *brujos,* or South American witch-doctors, flew to Iquitos in Peru and from there made his way on foot through the 'dense primeval forest of the upper Amazon' in search of these unusual jungle practitioners. Taking with him as guide, a Jivaro Indian called Gabrio, his search at first proved fruitless, and then . . .

JUNGLE DENTISTRY

. . . there was the matter of Gabrio's toothache. He had been complaining about it for two days, and when I told him that I was a tooth doctor he shook his head violently.

He was a wizened little man, with narrow shoulders, a pot belly and a disproportionately large head surmounted by a tangled mat of straight, black hair. I had purchased him, in a sense, from the patron of the rubber camp on the Morona River; that is, I had left a small camera and some film as a deposit until I should return Gabrio to him. Gabrio's cheerful grinning face and unfailing good humour had won my admiration and almost my affection, if such a sentiment can be said to exist towards a hideously painted savage whose relatives and immediate antecedents were head hunters.

In this barbarously cruel and treacherous country, a friendly face was like manna from heaven, however. Gabrio supplied not only human companionship but also the physical comforts of my existence, attending to all my wants—such as setting my hammock and arranging the mosquito netting at night; squatting in front of a small fire to watch for jaguars—or tigres, as they are called—and slithering ten-foot snakes; preparing stews made of well-cooked wild pig meat, tree rodents, and a few feathered friends we killed in the forest.

He also supplied certain spiritual comforts; for although we were somewhat apart in means of communication, since I could not speak much of his language and he knew only a few words of mine, we had learned to talk by signs and grunts. We had gone quite a few miles up the tributary river from the Upper Marañón, and were now headed back again; and I had learned to depend on Gabrio's knowledge of the country and the habits of the Indians to see me through safely.

Below us the wide Marañón lay like a flat yellow snake on the immense green blanket of seemingly endless jungles, draining off the concealed water from the marshes. Once I reached the Marañón I could probably make my way downriver to Iquitos again, perhaps on one of the river steamboats which infrequently traverse the river up as far as the Morona, carrying rubber hunters and their equipment.

I had asked Gabrio for information about any of the brujos

A witch-doctor prepares a potion.

he might have been acquainted with, but either he misunderstood me or professed ignorance as a result of fear. On this morning, however, the pain in his jaw seemed to outweigh all other problems. His eyes shone feverishly under the tangled mat of black hair, and now and then he pressed his fist against his jaw and clawed at the lower lip, as if to show the source of his agony.

'Look, Gabrio,' I said, with some exasperation. 'Me doctor! Fix tooth!'

I tried, with signs and the few words of his tribal dialect that I knew, to make him understand that I could probably relieve him. He merely shook his head again, gnashing his teeth as if he would crush the offending pain in his jaw.

'White man's magic not good for Indian,' he muttered. 'Me see doctor.'

He pronounced it 'dogeetah', something like dogeater, and after a moment of puzzlement I realised he wanted to see a witch-doctor. He was pointing to the river bank, where I could see traces of an Indian village.

My time was growing short. If we did not reach Iquitos before the heavy rains, I might be held up for weeks and would miss my plane for Belém, on the East Coast, where I had a connection through to Philadelphia. Gabrio's stubborn attitude was annoying; yet I knew he could not travel with his tooth in such a condition, so there was nothing to do but put in at the village.

Gabrio quickly routed out the 'dogeetah'. He was a thin, emaciated old man with an expression of wisdom and craftiness, which is almost a professional trademark of witch-doctors. It is hard to describe the particular qualities of this expression, which is sensed rather than seen. In succeeding years I would see these fellows perform in many places: in West Africa, Malaya, and New Guinea; but this was the only time I would ever come to one with a patient seeking dental help. It seemed a bit ridiculous; yet I was aware of the complete faith Gabrio had in this man, although he was from another tribe and I doubt if Gabrio had met him before.

I began to understand why Gabrio had turned down my offer of help. It was not lack of respect for the 'white man's magic'. All Indians had that respect, and some of them hate white men because of the respect they have for his powers. This was something else: not lack of faith in me, but absolute, unquestioning faith in the witch-doctor. This was evident in the manner of each as Gabrio chattered in his tribal dialect, making gestures and exposing a row of grimy unsightly teeth.

The village practitioner nodded gravely; and I observed that he

The medicine man of an aboriginal tribe performs a ceremonial blood-letting with an ox-horn and various stones and leaves.

was also watching me. Gabrio waved in my direction once or twice, perhaps explaining that I was a 'white doctor' and the old man nodded each time. There was no professional envy in his glance. It was a calculating, practical sort of appraisal.

I knew I was in for the time lost during the professional visit, and I prepared to watch with some interest the techniques to be employed. The strange ministrations of witch-doctors always interested me, and this afforded me a rare opportunity of witnessing the entire performance intimately. I would be able to watch the things from a ringside seat, like a visiting surgeon observing a colleague in the arena.

As events will show, Gabrio either did not have a toothache— or he had one that would have defied the best of modern dentists. As I watched Gabrio's man of medicine prepare for the practice of his queer art, I realised—possibly for the first time with any conscious perception of its importance—how completely Gabrio accepted the man's craft, with all its odd and ridiculous facets. Call it faith; or call it credulity. What ever it was, it was a variety of what we often refer to as 'psychotherapy' or the science of mental healing.

Gabrio's glittering eyes began to soften as soon as the witch-doctor took over. The native practitioner was tall for his tribe, with a wrinkled, ancient visage, and sharp, knowing eyes. He paid little attention to the sanitary formalities common to the simplest medical treatment. He did not wash his hands; and from the appearance of his hands, I doubted if he had ever performed this pre-operative ceremony. There was no dental chair, of course. He merely directed Gabrio to sit on the ground, and squatted in front of him, taking Gabrio's head between his knees.

Gabrio opened his mouth, exposing a cavernous array of stained, probably infected, teeth. The local doctor shoved one grimy fist into Gabrio's mouth, holding the back of Gabrio's head with the other hand, and prying open his jaws with sheer force. Gabrio grunted, but seemed to accept this rather abrupt diagnostic intimacy in good faith. About all that was left of his face, besides his mouth, were two beady eyes that peered confidently above the bridge of his flat nose. Two probing fingers nudged around the inflamed side of his gums, and the medicine man grunted with satisfaction—although what he had learned from this rough diagnosis I could not imagine.

A boy, apparently an apprentice, brought a bowl filled with a filthy-looking liquid. The witch-doctor bent over this, murmuring some kind of incantations. Meanwhile, his eyes were fixed on

Gabrio with a hypnotic stare. His body swayed slightly as he murmured his 'prayers'.

The witch-doctor suddenly reached for the bowl, swooped it to his face and gulped down the liquid. It was not at all surprising to me when he immediately retched and vomited the contents on the ground. My own professional sense, gained over years of practice, had become so numbed by the procedure thus far that I was more curious than horrified.

The witch-doctor, who must have been at least sixty which is old for an Indian, waved his hand as a signal for another bowl. The bowl was brought to him, and he repeated the process. As to what was being accomplished by this internal medication— not upon the patient, but upon the person of the doctor—I could only conjecture. But there was no doubt of its outward effect upon Gabrio. Gabrio was staring with fascinated attention at the local practitioner, and the latter had assumed a rapt, almost ecstatic expression. He signalled with his hand to his assistant, and the next instant the assistant whirled Gabrio over so that he was lying on the ground, his face upward. The witch-doctor kneeled above him, holding Gabrio's head firmly between his knees.

Once again he thrust his hand halfway into Gabrio's mouth; and at the same time he began to chew furiously on a tobacco-like bag he had taken into his own mouth, spitting on the ground first on one side of Gabrio, and then on the other. All the while he muttered over and over the words of the strange chant, in a weird, monotone rhythm.

The entire affair might have been amusing, had it not been for the fierce intensity of the old fellow's manner. He was going about this as seriously as any surgeon performing a critical operation.

I remained a few feet away, watching the performance with growing interest. I was not unacquainted with the basic precepts of native sorcery—particularly the need of establishing a rapport of absolute confidence between the practitioner and the patient. The complete faith with which Gabrio submitted to the Indian 'doctor's' ministrations, to the intimacies inside his mouth, would have served as an object lesson in the proper relationship between patient and physician in our more civilised society.

Suddenly the witch-doctor leaned forward and put his mouth against Gabrio's swollen cheek. He began to suck, furiously and noisily. The area was obviously tender, and Gabrio howled in agony; but the witch-doctor continued to suck at his cheek, his assistant helping to keep Gabrio's head firmly wedged against the ground.

Finally he raised his head and spat out something. I stepped closer and observed that it was a splinter of wood. How he had gotten it into his mouth I did not know; but I was sure it had not come through Gabrio's cheek. The old man looked around, uttering some sharp words in his native tongue, which I assumed referred to the result of his treatment.

Gabrio raised his head to stare at the offending splinter, but the old man shoved his head back on the ground again rather roughly, and resumed his sucking.

His next expectoration was a mouthful of ants. I became absorbed in the legerdemain. The old man seemed to have passed these things unobserved into his mouth; and when the third spitting produced a grasshopper, and the fourth a lizard, I became more than curious. The lizard was the *pièce de résistance*. He dangled it proudly by the tail, showing it to the other Indians who crowded around the pair.

Gabrio was permitted to sit up, and the medicine-man appeared to question him as to how he felt, with these offending objects out of his teeth. Gabrio felt rather gingerly at his cheek, and nodded; but from his expression and the few words I understood, I gathered that the tooth still ached.

At this point the medicine-man began to paw among the objects he had spat out on the ground. Both the grasshopper and the lizard were dead; and suddenly he pointed to the lizard. One leg had been severed from its body.

This seemed to call for a more serious plan of attack. The medicine man obtained a small bivalve shell from his assistant, and using the shell—a river mussel—as a pair of tweezers, he plucked a live coal from a near-by fire. He handed this to Gabrio, and for an instant I thought he was going to make Gabrio eat the live coal. But he quickly made it plain that Gabrio was merely to place the shell, with the coal inside it, in his mouth. The medicine man meanwhile mixed some dry leaves into an ash-like powder, and sprinkled the crumbled substance over the coal. It gave off a hot, penetrating aroma, something like bay leaves; and he helped Gabrio hold this in his mouth so that the fumes curled around his teeth.

After a few minutes Gabrio's expression relaxed. The pain left his tooth in a matter of a few seconds, and he turned to me happily and announced:

'Lizard claw smoke out tooth!'

This simple explanation settled matters as far as Gabrio was concerned. His pain was gone. It was 'smoked out'.

As we prepared to continue our journey downriver, I asked

Gabrio if he would permit me to examine his tooth. I wanted to see the extent or type of infection that seemed to have caused the trouble, and if possible relate it to the witch-doctor's fantastic performance. Gabrio either did not understand my request, or pretended not to understand it. He merely shrugged and said in somewhat jumbled explanation:

'Dogeetah he find lizard. He make sick.'

The notion that the lizard had taken over the 'spirit' of sickness that had caused the pain in Gabrio's tooth was not unusual. I have witnessed many witch-doctors performing rituals since then, and I know that in each case sickness or even death is never attributed to disease as we understand it, but to a 'bad spirit'. It is the task of the witch-doctor to locate that spirit and destroy or at least neutralise it.

Before leaving the village I secured some of the powdered leaves which the witch-doctor had used in the heated mussel shell. I intended to make an analysis of the leaves to see if they possessed some healing or anaesthetic property. They did not. They were a variety of the barbassu plant, with the properties of rotenone, which is used in a powerful insecticide. Apparently the leaves contained nothing that would cure a toothache or ease pain.

Witness to Witchcraft, by Harold B. Wright.

In medieval times people believed that leprosy could be cured by washing the sores with water containing mulberry or strawberry juice and that a toothache would disappear if the person suffering from it said 'argidam margidam sturgidam' and then spat into a frog's mouth.*

Have you any friends or relatives who have been cured by unorthodox means?

It is a well known fact that, with certain symptoms, if the patient has enough faith in the healing powers of the doctor, he will get better, regardless of what treatment is prescribed. A bottle of coloured water is an excellent tonic if we believe that it will do us good. Faith can move mountains. Gabrio was brought up in a society where belief in the healing power of the witch-doctor goes unchallenged. Was Gabrio's cure simply a question of mind over matter? Or did the witch-doctor pull Gabrio's tooth out when he first put his hand in his mouth?

The witch-doctor who cured Gabrio was a practitioner of white witchcraft in that he healed the sick, but there are those who practise the black arts, those whose skills are dedicated to the pursuit of evil . . .

In 1952 James H. Neal was appointed Chief Investigations Officer

* *Medieval Man*, by Frederick Harrison.

In rural Ghana, a man stabs himself repeatedly without drawing blood in demonstration of alleged protection by Ewe, a god of war.

for the Government of Ghana, in Accra. The nature of his work made him many enemies, some of whom contacted powerful witch-doctors in an attempt to prevent him from investigating their crimes. After several threats and warnings, Neal became very ill and was admitted to Accra hospital. His doctor diagnosed a virus infection and he was given anti-biotics but he knew that these were ineffective against the black spell that had been cast upon him by a powerful Ju-ju priest. His condition deteriorated and his friends, fearful for his life, suggested that a Moslem holy man, a Malam, called Alargi be sent for. The Malam visited Neal at his bedside and by means of rites and invocations broke the evil charm and placed a protective spell around his bungalow. Neil quickly recovered.

Soon, however, further attempts were made on his life by the powerful Ju-ju priests and once again Malam Alargi was contacted. The Malam told him that he was only protected while in his bungalow and to gain complete protection he would have to wear a special amulet next to his skin during the day and at night he would have to sleep with it under his pillow. Malam Alargi fashioned the amulet from parts of an elephant, a wild dog, a hyena, a lion, and a leopard. It was shaped like a large polished chestnut and cost Neal £50. He wore it continually and felt that the £50 had been well-spent because he was no longer troubled by the spells of the Ju-ju priests, that is until . . .

BAD THINGS ON BLACK SATURDAY

Most people have experienced days on which things have been so catastrophic as to sear themselves into their memory for all time. Such a day for me was September 8th 1962. It was a day I desperately want to forget. But it was a day that left marks on my body which will for ever remind me of that black Saturday.

I went to bed early the night before. I knew that Saturday was going to be a heavy day, and I wanted to leave early for the office. There was a huge backlog of administrative work to slog through and get finished before leaving for the racecourse, and I wanted to get there before the races started. Not that I was setting myself up for a pleasant afternoon's gambling. Although I was a member of the Turf Club and thoroughly enjoyed a day at the races, this particular jaunt was to be purely in the line of duty.

Accra Racecourse was one of the best I had ever seen. The whole thing was organised on strictly business-like and efficient lines, and it was financially strong and well kept, it was a credit to the city. Occasionally blots came in the form of doping inci-dents, with their attendant smells and screams of 'fixing'. But the big money behind this form of crime made it highly attractive to syndicates and avaricious individuals alike.

JUNGLE WITCHCRAFT

The lure of what Americans call 'the fast buck' is very strong indeed, and there are few locations more likely to attract people who have, again to quote our American friends, 'their eye on the main chance'. On many a balmy afternoon, therefore, I was able temporarily to end the freedom of citizens who were trying to add to their gains by strictly illegal means.

I mean it was odds on that if you saw a lowly Government official, a poorly paid clerk, a labourer, or a layabout playing the part of a free-spender with the bookies, you were also looking at someone about whom there was something gravely suspicious. Dig the earth, and you'll find worms. Dissect a suspicious-seeming gambler, and you'll often uncover embezzlement, fraud, or extortion.

Saturday, September 8th 1962, was a day on which Adjei, four other officers, and myself were going to pay a visit to the race meeting with the intention of hauling in certain unsavoury characters we suspected of race-fixing. We had a hot tip-off that they would be there, and we wanted to arrive early to spot our suspects.

This then was the background to the day on which my alarm-clock failed to go off. When I did wake up I was furious to find that I was behind the schedule I had prepared on Friday night. I felt like slinging the clock hard against the nearest wall. Shaving in a hurry, I nicked my face, and fought an endless and futile battle against the blood which threatened to pour down my chin and on to my shirt.

In the bathroom, bent double over the washbasin, I suddenly decided to see whether in fact the alarm-clock's failure to function hadn't been my fault for not winding and setting it. I rushed back into the room and lifted the timepiece from its customary place on the bedside table. It had been wound and was still set. It just hadn't gone off.

More infuriated than ever, I pulled out a change of clothing, dressed, and gulped down a few mouthfuls of breakfast. Then away into Accra.

The phone hardly stopped ringing all through the morning, and every second call, it seemed, had to be dealt with by me. By the time we were ready to leave for the racecourse I could cheerfully have tied a landmine to the blasted clock that had let me down so badly.

The gang we were hoping to apprehend had infiltrated right into the running of the day's races. Stableboys, jockeys, grooms —all were implicated in some way or other. This crowd certainly was playing for high stakes.

When we got to the racecourse, I dispersed Adjei and the others to strategic points, then went high up to a corner of the new grandstand to get a bird's-eye view. I wanted to see from up there that everything would work according to our pre-race briefing session. From where I stood I could see right down over the whole area. As it was still early very few people had come into this stand, and those that were there were standing in a little cluster about twenty yards from my vantage-point.

This was great. I was alone with nobody near me, and I could watch clearly everything that was going on. After a while I picked out the suspects in the crowd, and even as I watched my officers began to close in. It was like a military operation, and was very thrilling for me to see. When the suspects were completely surrounded and the arrests were just about to be made I decided to go down so that I could start the interrogation as soon as possible.

Suddenly, as I turned to walk down the steps, I was pushed violently from the rear. I began to plummet downwards, and in the fraction of a second before I plunged down from the grandstand level I twisted my head back to see who had shoved me. There was nobody there. I was hurtling down towards the ground my whole body already screaming in anticipation of the pain. Then it seemed that a huge explosion of light went off behind my eyeballs, there was an instant of agony, then—blackness. Nothing. No feeling. No existence.

When I opened my eyes I could see nothing other than vague shapes swimming in front of my eyes. There was a moment of panic when I thought I was going blind. I shut my eyes again and tried to remember what had happened, where I was. But again, nothing. I couldn't feel my hands or feet or any part of my body. I opened my eyes again, and for the first time heard voices. Then out of the swimming, gyrating shapes in front of me a face slowly materialised. At first I had no idea who this man was.

Then he said, 'That's it. That's a good chap. You're all right. Don't worry.'

I tried to speak. I couldn't get the words to come out, and the effort was so exhausting that I felt myself slipping away again. I didn't fight it. The blackness came down again all over me, enshrouding, cushioning, and very comforting. I let it happen.

Eventually I came to again, I don't know how much later, but this time there was pain all down my left side. Through the arm it throbbed, and along the side of my body and right down into my leg. This time when I opened my eyes I could see, and the same man was there. This time I recognised him. He was a doctor, and I was in hospital. I remembered now exactly what had happened on the grandstand at the racecourse.

'Feel better now?' the doctor asked.

'I feel alive,' I said. 'I don't know that I feel better, but at least I can feel something. Incidentally, am I talking? Can you hear me? Am I making sense?'

'Yes, you're talking, and I can hear you, and you are making sense,' the doctor replied. 'And I might add that you're a lucky man to be alive.'

'What are my injuries?' I said. 'I feel as if I'm all smashed up.'

'You've had a fair old knocking about, but don't worry—we'll patch you up all right.'

'But tell me exactly what's wrong,' I said.

'Well, your left arm and leg have multiple fractures for a start,' he said. 'And there are various other injuries down your left side which we don't have to go into now. The main thing is not to worry too much about it. Just try to concentrate on getting better. We'll do our part, but a lot depends on you too, you know. Now try to get some rest. If there is anything you want the nurse will get it for you.'

With that he left the room. I lay back and thought over what had happened. Who could have pushed me? I wondered. There certainly hadn't been anyone within sixty feet of me. I remembered distinctly looking behind me a few seconds before I made up my mind to go down to join my officers. There had been nobody close to me. And yet that shove had been violent.

The stray thought that it might have been a Ju-ju attack flitted across my mind, but vanished immediately when I remembered that I was fully protected by the amulet Malam Alargi had given me. But that amulet, where was it?

I called the nurse, and when she arrived I asked her if my suit was handy.

'Yes, it is here in the wardrobe,' she said.

'I wonder if you would bring it over to me, please?' I asked. She looked puzzled, but brought the suit over to my bed.

With my good hand, the right one, I searched in the pocket where the amulet usually lay. There was no amulet there. I tried another pocket, and another. I went through all of them. There was no amulet.

'Have you lost something, Mr Neal?' the nurse asked.

'Has anyone taken anything out of these pockets?' I asked in answer.

'Taken anything? No, sir. Your suit hasn't been touched

since it was taken off you when you were brought in in the ambulance. Why, have you lost something?'

'No, it is all right thank you, nurse,' I said. 'Perhaps you'd be kind enough to put the suit back.'

She hung the suit up in the little wardrobe, and after fussing around for a few minutes went out and left me alone again. I tried to figure out about the amulet, and then I remembered. Of course, I had left in such a rush because of the clock's failure to wake me that I must have forgotten to transfer the amulet from under my pillow, where I always kept it at night.

Adjei came in some time later. He stood at the end of the bed for a few seconds, shaking his head slowly in an eloquent gesture of sympathy.

'It is terrible to see you like this, sir,' he said.

'Thanks, Adjei,' I said. 'But don't mind me. What time of day is it? And what happened—did you get all the suspects?'

'It's about five o'clock in the afternoon, sir. Yes, we caught them all. They're all being detained now, awaiting trial. We've got everything we want to get them a good, stiff sentence each.

'Thank God for that much,' I said, relieved. 'At least something went right. Even if it did cost me this little package of trouble.'

'I don't understand it, sir,' Adjei said. 'It was as if you were pushed over the top.'

'Oh, you actually saw it then?' I asked him.

'Yes, sir, I was looking towards you at the time.'

'And what exactly did you see?'

'You turned and looked behind you. Then you looked down at us again, standing still for a moment. Then, just as you took your first step, it looked exactly as if someone had caught you and pushed you hard right over the top. But there was nobody there to push you.'

'Are you quite sure there was nobody close to me?'

'There was nobody near you at all, sir. I should say the nearest people to you were, well, it's difficult to say from where I was, but I would estimate fifteen, maybe twenty, yards away.'

So I hadn't been wrong!

'In fact, sir,' Adjei went on, 'if I didn't know that you were well protected by your amulet I would have said that you were attacked by Ju-ju.'

I told him then that I had forgotten it. He was aghast, and insisted on going to fetch it straight away.

He was back in less than an hour with it, having found it under my pillow where I had left it.

'You must never, ever forget to have it with you, sir,' he said. 'Here, please keep it under your pillow now. It is your only protection.'

Once again I was very moved by Adjei's concern for me. We had grown very close to each other in the ten years in which I had been his superior at the investigations office. He was always so loyal and solicitious, and such an intelligent officer.

Next morning the nurse came and told me there was a visitor waiting to see me. I asked her to show the visitor in, and I was very surprised when Malam Alargi was ushered in. He too showed deep concern at my state, looking with awe and sympathy at the plaster of Paris that seemed to encase most of my body. After some preliminary chat he said, 'I have read the oracle for you, and from the sand and the stones and the beads I have seen that a big enemy of yours went to a very Big Ju-ju man and asked him to kill you.'

'So that's what happened,' I said.

'Not quite, because this Ju-ju man could not harm you because of the amulet I made for you. He decided to try something else. He stopped your alarm-clock from ringing and waking you.'

This was astonishing. I had not mentioned to anyone about the clock. Not to my servant, not to Adjei. And here was the Malam telling me! He just smiled when I told him that he was right, and that I was stunned.

'This Ju-ju man also succeeded in confusing your mind,' he went on. 'He put your mind in such a turmoil that when you left your bungalow to drive to your office you forgot to get your amulet out from under your pillow.'

I shouldn't have said it, but I blurted out, 'You have been talking to Adjei, haven't you? He told you.'

The Malam's face clouded with hurt. I thought for a moment he was going to get up and leave. He looked at me with eyes that made me want to squirm with shame. Then: 'I have not seen Adjei for many long months. Do you think I would want to resort to such low trickery?'

I didn't answer, only because I was too ashamed. I shook my head.

'I heard about your accident from a news bulletin,' he went on, 'and went immediately to read the oracle. I have other things to tell you, but perhaps you would wish me to go since you seem to doubt me?'

'Please don't go,' I said. 'I'm sorry about what I said. It's just that it is so amazingly accurate as to be uncanny. No, I'd like you to tell me what you read in the oracle.'

Malam Alargi smiled and continued to tell me what else he had read.

'When this very Big Ju-ju man saw from reading his own oracle that you had left behind your amulet and were not protected by it, he summoned an entity from the astral level to be around you. I saw from the oracle that this entity, which you probably did not see, pushed you, and I also saw you falling a long distance down.'

He looked at me penetratingly.

'You must never again be without your amulet, my friend, as otherwise they will kill you! I have brought you another medicine which you must always carry with you or keep at night under your pillow, and this special medicine will make any future attempts to confuse your mind impossible.'

When I inquired what I owed him he replied, slightly offended, that he would not accept a penny piece. He had done it as an act of sincere friendship. I felt overwhelmed by the kindness of this man who, during the past years, had become such a good friend to me.

Jungle Magic, by James H. Neal.

Was it just coincidence, do you think, that nothing happened to Neal while he was wearing his amulet?

Neal says he 'was pushed violently in the rear' and before he fell he turned 'to see who had shoved' him, but 'there was nobody there.' Could it have been a heavy object, thrown by one of his enemies, which shoved him down the steps? Adjei did say there were people within twenty yards of him before he fell. He turned expecting to see the person who had pushed him. Could he have overlooked the missile lying at his feet? Or do you believe, with Malam Alargi, that it was an 'entity from the astral level' (in other words a ghost summoned up by a Ju-ju priest) that attacked him?

James Neal relied upon Malam Alargi to free him from the curses of the Ju-ju priests. On the other hand Major Court-Treatt decided to challenge a witch-doctor himself, by playing him at his own game.

DUEL BY WITCHCRAFT

A duel to the death proved the only way to settle matters between myself and the foul witch-doctor called 'the Karogi'.

The year was 1921 and my native trackers and I had established a rest camp in Bandala country along the border between Sudan and French Equatorial Africa. We had camped to rest, refit, and explore ahead for the next year's hunting which I proposed to do in the little-known Koreish Divide.

JUNGLE WITCHCRAFT

I had no intention of becoming involved in local matters at all. I meant to enjoy leisurely discussions with the young chief and the very intelligent Fiki, or chief priest, of the Arabic-speaking Bandalas. But Fate over-ruled me and I was soon empaneled to serve as a grim and primitive coroner's jury deep in the forest.

One morning just before dawn the chief of the Bandalas came secretly to my tent and told me of the cruel death of a young girl of the village. The young chief, brave but obviously terrified, begged me as a friend to come with him and the girl's parents to 'see what I would see'.

The girl, he said, had left home to become a servant to the Karogi, the local practitioner of black magic. Now she had been found dead, apparently mauled by a hyena.

The Karogi was a member of the Karogi tribe who, ten years before, had wandered into Bandala country and built himself a hut in a dense thicket in the forest. He soon became known simply as 'the Karogi'. Gradually there had arisen around him, like a foul miasma, a reputation for evil, black magic, and spells. He admitted he was a witch-doctor but he preyed on the people and practised extortion by imbuing them with fears and threats. He demanded excessive gifts for his services and it was said that anyone who opposed his wishes fell sick and died.

I joined the funeral party, taking with me some of my boys— tough, hardened hunters who had shared many experiences with me.

We came to a little clearing in the forest where the body of the girl lay. A short distance off, in the shade, sat the Karogi, wrapped in a filthy, evil-smelling skin robe. It covered the whole of his body and almost all of his face, but from the fold over his head his eyes gleamed out at us. He was silent and motionless.

We approached and looked down at the body of the young girl. On the ground, which was sandy, was the undoubted spoor (tracks) of hyena pads. The body was terribly torn and mauled.

Now a hunter with years of experience in the far places must, perforce at times, have seen bodies mauled by wild animals. As I gazed at the pathetic remains, I had a strong feeling that there was something wrong, something unnatural. I called to Koh Kong, my little bushman tracker, and gave him, surreptitiously, the bushman sign which means 'look carefully'.

That night after dinner I summoned Koh Kong and gave him tobacco for his little black pipe and he squatted, puffing at my feet. Now, Koh Kong is the best tracker I have ever had. His powers were uncanny. He could run on spoor in dry grass which I could not see even when it was shown to me. Above all, he had the art of sensing or seeing subconsciously thousands of small signs which gave him a true picture of what had happened.

For awhile I let Koh Kong smoke his pipe in peace and then suddenly I said, 'Koh Kong, was the girl killed by a hyena?'

He looked at me for a second, his eyes were mere pinpoints and then shot out his hands, fingers extended. This is the sign for warding off evil. Then he rose, turned rapidly and left. I knew that I would not get one word out of him, but I had my answer.

Very shortly word drifted through to my boys and so to me of the Karogi witch-doctor's enmity. Possibly my slight training in medicine and surgery by which I was able to cure minor ills earned his jealousy, for naturally I charged nothing and he must have felt that I was not only robbing him of his fees but also whittling down his prestige.

I did not take the witch-doctor's enmity lightly; magic or trickery, call it what you will, can be dangerous and it seemed that his tricks and spells began to work. At first it was odd things, small things, but yet annoying. Little objects disappeared. Water jars were found leaking. Tent pegs were pulled from the ground with only the strain of a slight wind and tents fell.

I became anxious and annoyed when things started happening to my pets. It has long been my habit while hunting to catch animals and train them. In this camp I had a baby giraffe, several species of buck, half a dozen gazelles, some monkeys, several maribou storks, demoiselle cranes, and various other animals. Several of these animals just disappeared.

One of the storks was found with a broken leg and had to be destroyed. Two of the monkeys unexplainably were found hanging limply over the branches of a small tree, apparently poisoned. Then the compound where the large animals were kept was raided several times at night—apparently by hyenas—and several of my pet gazelles disappeared.

My suggestion that one or two of the boys should mount guard over the animal pen was received with cold fear. They seemed ashamed to refuse and answered with downcast eyes, but I did not feel entitled to press the point.

For three or four weeks nothing further happened and we heard that the Karogi had gone on a journey. Then news was brought that he had returned and that he had another servant to replace the poor girl who had been killed. This servant was a boy.

One day soon after we got this news I was sitting outside my tent while Achmad, the head boy, was clipping my hair. While he was doing this I was paring my nails. As we talked I noticed a strange-looking small boy, wandering dreamily about the camp. Twice previously he had asked me for work but I told him there was none for him and dismissed him with a small present. I noticed him now, squatted not far from my tent and I studied him. He looked about seven or eight years old and was thin and dirty. His face was utterly expressionless and his eyeballs seemed fixed; the pupils enlarged and clouded like muddy pools.

My hair finished, I looked around for the tent boy and then remembered that I had sent him on an errand. So I called the little boy with the strange face and, pointing out a broom and a flat basket, told him to sweep up the hair and throw it on the fire about fifty yards from the camp. This fire always was kept smouldering for the burning of rubbish.

I sat down and was studying a map of the Divide when I heard a yell.

Jerking my head up, I saw the small boy running hard for the forest with Baballa, our expert elephant hunter, behind him. The boy tripped and fell but was up in a flash and streaked into the shades of the forest.

After a little Baballa returned. To my surprise, I saw that he was back-tracking himself with infinite care; suddenly he stopped and bent over, gazing at the ground. He looked towards camp and, seeing me watching him, waved to me to join him. I walked over. Wordlessly he pointed to where the little boy had stumbled. He had dropped a few tufts of my hair and a nail clipping or two, but must have gotten off into the forest with quite a handful.

Baballa told me this small boy must be the servant of the witch-doctor. We looked at each other and I am not ashamed to say that I was scared. This was a type of magic of which I had heard.

However, for a week or so, I was busy planning the new season's hunting and had not much time to think of witchcraft. But I noticed my boys watched me more attentively than usual.

Then I began to feel weak and ill. It is hard to describe the sickness which came upon me so gradually. It started with just a feeling of laziness. This got worse; every day I felt a little weaker. At first I hoped it might be sandfly fever but soon knew it was not.

I had to admit that I was faced with the allegedly impossible. I knew the Karogi had used my hair and nail parings, probably in a clay model, in order to work some vile black magic upon me.

I stirred my sluggish brain and fading energy to the point where I made up my mind to fight fire with fire.

I have quite a skill in modelling, so I had clay and bamboo brought to the store hut which always was kept locked and which was just behind my tent. Locked in the sweaty gloom of the hut I made a framework, or armature as sculptors call it, from the bamboo, and on this frame I constructed a life-size dummy of the Karogi.

This dummy finished, I summoned Baballa, Koh Kong, Achmad, and Jamahala my chief hunter. All of them had been with me for years; they knew me and I knew them as my faithful friends. I swore them to complete secrecy and we made a plan.

First we must entice the Karogi away from his hut. So I persuaded the young chief to send a message to the Karogi, saying he wished to consult him on a profitable but very secret matter. It was so secret in fact that he must meet him alone, at the rise of the moon, at a ford some three miles from the Karogi's hut.

This message was carefully framed to appeal to the Karogi's avariciousness.

Later we got word the Karogi had agreed. The chief was told not to keep the appointment but to remain in his hut and he seemed happy not to come in personal contact with the Karogi.

That night, a dark night, my four boys and I wrapped the dummy of Karogi in a cloth and stole out of the camp by a back trail. A little distance along the trail to our surprise, we found my friend the Fiki waiting. He said no word but joined us and his muttered prayers and incantations seemed to hearten my boys and even to encourage me, for I was now very weak and shaking as though with malaria. I acted in a dream. Only my will-power kept me going.

Eventually we arrived near the Karogi's hut. Koh Kong stole forward and returned reporting all was clear. We went up to the hut and cut the leather lashings of the door and entered.

My flashlight showed strange objects piled up in corners and slung from the roof poles. There were greasy leather bags of unknown contents. There were bones and dried entrails of animals, strips of hides and claws (apparently hyenas') strung on a brilliant scarlet rope. Above all, there was a vile and evil smell.

Baballa, whose eyes were darting everywhere, froze and pointed to a corner of the hut. There was a foot-high replica, made out of an old bit of canvas, of a tent.

I stepped forward to move it but the Fiki held me back. I

saw that he had brought with him a pair of wooden tongs. Later I learned these were made from the branches of the tree called Shiggra Beida, which means 'The White Tree'. If a branch of the tree is stirred in muddy water it will immediately clear it. I have used it since many times for clearing mud from wells or streams or water holes fouled by game. Because of its ability to clear water it has acquired a connotation of purity.

With these tongs the Fiki moved the tent and I was horrified, but not surprised, to see a devilishly clever wax figure of myself spread-eagled and pinned upon the ground with long needle-sharp thorns from the Tahl tree. These thorns are not only sharp, but somewhat poisonous; their prick causes an aching pain for hours.

My boys by now were huddled together and literally trembling with fear.

The Fiki touched nothing with his hands. With the tongs he removed the thorns one by one and placed them, together with the doll, in a piece of skin. All the while he recited prayers and finally tied the bundle tightly with thongs.

I now set about executing my plan. I was too weak and sluggish to do anything myself and my boys were sweating with fear, but such was their discipline and affection for me that they carried out what was to them a task so fearsome as to be almost impossible.

The effigy of the Karogi was slung by a rope from the roof poles. The hands were tied out sideways to wall poles of the hut and the feet were pegged to the ground with two sharpened stakes. From my haversack I produced four of the long razor-sharp hunting knives used by the Arabs. One, I drove to the hilt into the image between the eyes, one into the throat, one where the heart would be, and one into the stomach. All this was done in a great hurry for the Karogi might return at any moment.

As we left the foul smelling hut we tied the door exactly as it had been. The hinges had been cut but my boys cleverly faked them so that they looked good. However, when the door was opened, with no hinges, it would fall forward into the face of anyone trying to enter.

We quietly walked some half mile into the forest and there squatted nervously on the ground to wait.

Only the Fiki remained calm. He squatted, clutching his amulet (which held excerpts from the Koran) with one hand and my wrist with the other. His melodious monotone, praying continuously, was the only sound in the dark depths of the forest.

Koh Kong lifted his hand and gave the bushman sign for 'listen'. I heard nothing but it was obvious that Koh Kong and Baballa heard. Their eyes turned in the direction of the Karogi's hut.

Suddenly the night silence was rent by a succession of screams. Screams of horror, fear, rage, and terrible curses were followed by the sound of a body plunging wildly through the bush.

Almost immediately we saw a yellow glow from the direction of the Karogi's hut, followed by a sheet of red flame which rose above the tree-tops with sparks and whirling clouds of black smoke.

We sat and listened to the sounds of the Karogi thrashing about in the forest. Periodically we heard strange animal-like howls or a string of curses. There would be short periods of silence.

Suddenly we heard the most terrible prolonged scream of rage and fear that it ever has been my luck or misfortune to hear.

Then the Fiki, still holding me by the arm, and still reciting his prayers, began to move forward. I thought I now heard a note of thankfulness in his praying.

In a clearing of the forest we found the body of the Karogi. He lay spread-eagled on his back. The expression on his face defies description. His lips were drawn back in an animal snarl, showing yellow teeth. His eyes protruded, staring fixedly up at the dark sky. A great Arab hunting knife had been driven through his heart, pinning him to the ground.

The Fiki now took complete command. Two of the boys were sent, running, to camp for spades. On their return a shallow grave was dug. Using the spades the Karogi's body was pushed into the grave and poles thrown on top. The Fiki sharpened a stake some six feet long from a branch of the white Shiggra Beida, peeled the bark from it, lifted it high and with one tremendous surge, drove it through the body of the Karogi and into the ground. Then branches and windfalls were piled into an immense funeral pyre.

A light was set to this pyre and as the flames rose the skin containing the wax image of me was placed against the white pole.

We watched the flames rise in wavering curtains of fire, then burn lower and lower until only a red-hot bed of coals remained. I saw with amazement that the white pole stood almost unscorched and intact.

Silent and strained by our terrible night we started the short trek back to camp. As we walked I realised that a change was coming over my whole body. It was like a drink of old French brandy. The world seemed alive again and I was returning to it.

The Strange and the Unknown,
by Major C. Court-Treatt, as told to Helen R. Hunger.

Why did the white man's dummy have such a strange effect upon the Karogi?

Major Court-Treatt does not tell us who caused the Karogi's death, only that 'a great Arab hunting knife had been driven through his heart, pinning him to the ground.' Was it suicide? Or was it murder? And if it was murder, who do you think killed the Karogi?

Is black witchcraft based solely upon fear? Does the victim, learning that a witch-doctor has placed a spell upon him, quite literally scare himself to death?

Of all the unusual stories of witchcraft, black magic, and Ju-ju that have come out of Africa, perhaps the strangest concerns the incredible events witnessed by Administrative Officer Frank Hives, the weird tale of 'the rope man of Isuingu', or . . .

THE HAUNTED REST HOUSE

I left my headquarters in the early morning and marched to a large village named Egugu, sixteen miles away, in which there was a native court. There I remained to await my carriers and my staff—which, as usual, consisted of the interpreter, a native police orderly, a lance-corporal and three native constables, two court messengers, and my three servants.

Nothing of any importance happened that night, and the people of the village were very friendly, while there were no cases of any importance to hear. So the next day I set out for another town called Isuingu, about seventeen miles further on.

According to the notes made in the intelligence book by my predecessor, this place had none too good a reputation. The population was given as about eight hundred, and the three principal chiefs were stated to be 'very unintelligent' and inclined to resent any interference with the affairs of their town. The roads were stated to be bad, water bad, and the rest house (built two years before during the occupation of the country by the troops) bad. The date given in the book showed that Isuingu had been visited by the political officer just twelve months before.

Judging that after so long a time the rest house—native built, of course—would need some repairing and cleaning up to make it at all habitable, I despatched one of the court messengers with instructions to the chiefs to have the place ready for me, also a supply of firewood and fresh water for my use. I did not anticipate that much in the way of repairs could be done in the time, and anticipated an uncomfortable stay because of the attitude of the people.

I left Egugu at half-past five in the morning and did the distance by eleven o'clock. Most of the route had lain through dense forest, but the last few miles of the road, if it could be called such, ran through many scattered compounds and was very heavy, being ankle-deep in loose sand. I was very hot, tired and, I may add, thirsty when at length I came to a large, sand-covered clearing on which a few odd oil-palms were growing. Then I saw what I judged to be the rest house, with barracks or quarters for my staff near by.

Coming away from this were two or three hundred natives of all ages and both sexes, who were armed with twig brooms, hoes, and matchets. Evidently my instructions regarding the cleaning up of the place had been carried out. But I noticed that none of the people looked cheerful, as most gangs do when carrying out a collective task, and also that those who passed me did not flash their teeth and eyes in smiling greeting. In fact they looked sulky and decidedly unfriendly. Later the court messenger who had conveyed my instructions to the chiefs told me that they had been most reluctant to comply with them, and to turn out their people to do the work. Also, though he had told them to be at the rest house to meet me, they had not come.

Another thing I noticed was that the carriers, after having deposited their loads on the veranda of the rest house, did not linger to put them in order, but went as quickly as they could to the places arranged for them to live in. Even the police appeared to be uneasy, and almost surly in their silence. But I put this down as the effect of the long and trying march over the sand and under the sun.

After a bath and lunch I sent for the chiefs, who presently appeared looking as though they would rather have been anywhere else. I asked them through the interpreter why they had not been at the rest house to meet me; but it was some time before I got a reply. Eventually one grey-headed patriarch stepped forward, and after having scratched nearly every part of his none too clean skin with black-rimmed, claw-like nails—making a sound like rough concrete being rubbed with sandpaper—said:

'We do not mean to be disrespectful; but we did not want you to come here—it means trouble.'

I questioned him, again through the interpreter; but was unable to elicit the nature of the trouble, so had to give it up.

That afternoon I visited the town and heard various complaints and palavers, returning to the rest house just before sunset to enter up my intelligence book and to note the various doings of the day in my diary. Then, after the evening meal—which was made unpleasant by the numerous flies—I prepared to turn in.

The rest house was of the usual bush-built type, having walls of red mud six feet in height, and a raffia palm-leaf roof. There were two rooms, separated by a wide, open passage. They were unceiled and the rafters of the roof met at the ridge-pole about fourteen feet above the floor, which was of smoothly beaten mud. Around the house ran mud and wattle walls about three feet six inches in height, with openings at intervals to give access to the veranda thus formed. The servants' quarters, kitchen hut, and staff quarters were about thirty yards away to the left, leaving a sandy, open space in front of the rest house.

As the sun set and the evening chill set in I became aware of a peculiarly unpleasant odour. It was not in any particular place but seemed to pervade the whole house. It was a smell difficult to describe, though at the time I thought it was like long-dead bodies.

I called my servants and told them to find the source of this smell, with the idea of doing away with it. They were anything but keen, seeming to dislike the job, and after a very perfunctory search reported to me that they could find nothing. Their manner in making this report conveyed to me that they had not expected to find anything, and that the search was useless. Also they kept glancing at each other in a half-scared way, and seemed eager to be gone.

I was anything but pleased with my surroundings. The smell was bad enough; but in addition to this there was an unnatural something about the place that gave me an eerie feeling. I found myself peering into the gloomy corners, though what I expected to see I could not have described. However, I pulled myself together and prepared for sleep.

I had had my camp-bed set up on the veranda, with the object of escaping as much of the smell as possible, its head to the wall of the house; and beside it was a small folding camp-table, on which stood a lamp. My deck chair, office box and another folding table were about eight paces away, near enough for me to hear if anyone interfered with them.

After having tucked the mosquito net under the mattress for me, my servants said good-night, and scampered off with what I thought quite unnecessary haste. Then I started to read for a spell before turning down the lamp, but could not settle down to it. There seemed to be what I might describe as 'inaudible' sounds going on, which made me sit up at intervals and listen—for what I could not have said.

Then I heard a knock on the corner of the veranda post, and saw my cook—a boy who had been about two years in my service—standing outside with a hurricane lantern in his hand. He seemed to be shaking with fear, looking over his shoulder at intervals as if he expected something to jump at him any moment. With his teeth chattering so that he could hardly speak, he said: 'Massa, I beg you, I beg you proper no sleep for dis place, he be bad place, make we go one time.'

This needed some explanation. So I got up and asked him what he meant by saying it was a 'bad place'. But he could only repeat what he had said, and then added, with a fearful glance over his shoulder: 'Plenty man die here, plenty bad t'ing live here.'

The first part of the statement I could well believe: the smell had become stronger and decidedly more 'corpsey'. I began to feel chilly, and also, I must admit, rather creepy. In fact, without admitting to myself that I was afraid, I would willingly have taken the boy's advice to sleep elsewhere had there been anywhere else to sleep. But I could hardly break camp at that time of night simply because I didn't like the place, or give as a reason that I was scared. My prestige would have fallen, and following that a lessening of my influence over the natives. So there was nothing to be done but stick it out and pray for sleep, or daylight.

I thought of calling for a couple of my native police to mount guard. But this again would have showed at once that I feared something, and might have caused a stampede of the whole of my staff. Besides, whatever it was that was responsible for the stench and the creepy feeling, it was not anything that the police could deal with.

The boy still stood shivering, evidently in the grip of real terror. The least noise would, I think, have made him faint, or die, on the spot. I summoned up my courage and told him not to be a damned fool, as there was nothing to be afraid of; and warned him that if anyone came monkeying round they would get a bullet or two in them.

He begged me not to blame him if anything dreadful happened, and to remember that he had warned me. I then pretended to be angry and told him to clear out. But my heart sank as I saw him spring across the sandy ground. Even he, scared though he was, had been welcome company, and as I heard him barricading himself in his hut I felt more lonely than ever, and wished heartily that he had not come, as he had communicated some of his panic to me.

I took up the lamp and made a tour round the house. Then I went through the two empty rooms. I saw nothing, but could not get away from the feeling that something was watching me. It seemed to be quite close to me when I was in the passage between the rooms, and further off when I went to the end of the veranda where my gear was, and for this I was thankful.

Then, after inspecting my revolver to see that it was loaded and in good working order, I placed it under my pillow and got into bed again, tucked the mosquito net well in, and lay down. The lamp was burning well and a box of matches lay near it. I trusted that the oil in it would last out the night, for if it were to go out during the night I should be in a very unpleasant position.

It was then just ten o'clock, and all noises from the neighbouring town had ceased. A flicker or two from the fires the carriers had lighted showed now and again, but they soon died down and the darkness outside was intense. The lamp illuminated a space of only a few feet around me, so that I seemed to be at the centre of a tiny oasis of light in the midst of a desert of black nothingness. Not a sound came from the servants' quarters, nor from the police huts. Either all were asleep or were lying in scared silence, huddling together probably so as to feel the touch of something human. Almost I could have envied them.

I wished I had had a fire lighted in front. But it was too late now; for to have called any of my people would have showed that I shared their fear, and that was what I could not afford to do. So I just lay on my back, staring into the screen of darkness, hoping to fall asleep and yet afraid to lose consciousness. Sleep would not come, however, and I tried to imagine what it was that made the place uncanny. That this feeling was not the result of my own imagination was proved by the fact that my people felt it, and not only them but the townsfolk as well. It seemed to account for the unwillingness of the chiefs to have me stay there, and for the lack of cheerfulness shown by the gang which had done the cleaning up. They were, of course, superstitious like all natives and probably easily scared. But in my case it was different. Many and many a time in my career I had slept alone in the bush, and I was certainly not given to superstitious beliefs. Had I not experienced the curious eerie feeling I might have put down their fear to some local legend; but now I knew there must be something more than that to account for it.

The stillness was appalling. I could have yelled with the horror of it. Even the crickets had ceased their chirping; all the world might have been dead. Hours seemed to elapse.

Then I must have felt drowsy, but could not say if I had dropped off to sleep. All I knew was that suddenly I was wide awake. What was that? I sat up—my hair bristling—my skin cold and clammy.

There was a noise at the end of the veranda where my deck chair and other gear were! I pulled up the mosquito curtain, grasping my revolver, and sat on the edge of the bed, endeavouring to pierce that infernal gloom. Everything was as before, nothing had stirred. Then—as I looked—the chair was drawn back to the wall, so that the leg rest fell with a clatter to the hard mud floor.

What could have caused the chair to move? Nothing was visible, and yet the little group of travelling kit was well within the oasis of light.

Then the table was suddenly moved to one side as though some invisible hand had dragged it, and the chair toppled right over! If only I could have seen something I would have fired at once and found out afterwards what it was. But there was nothing to shoot at. Strangely enough, too, I felt less scared now that something was actually happening. I rose to my feet and started to investigate, carrying the lighted lamp. There was nothing to be seen near the overturned chair. A stray pie dog from the town or even a bush cat might have caused the upset. But then I should probably have heard the scampering of the retreating animal.

Then I thought that perhaps some of the unfriendly natives of the town might be trying to scare me into going away. I set my teeth and vowed that he, or they, should have a sorry time if I caught any of them. Or perhaps it was the village 'craze' man. I waited—listening. But there was nothing.

Then I bethought me of an old trick I had seen practised. Stepping outside I gathered handfuls of fine dry sand and scattered it evenly and fairly thickly on the floor, around the place where the chair and table stood, and across the openings in the veranda wall, taking care to leave no marks on the surface. Any native, dog, cat, or any other animal walking over this would leave easily discernible tracks, and I would be able to find out what it was with which I had to contend.

Then I returned to my bed and sat down on it, to wait and watch, revolver at the ready.

For about ten minutes I sat there, though it seemed more like an hour, and no further movements occurred. I began to feel drowsy and longed to lie down to enjoy undisturbed sleep. In fact I was just on the point of doing so when the smell became more pronounced, seeming to drift across to me from the opening in the veranda wall at the foot of the bed. Stronger and stronger it grew until my stomach turned and I was nearly sick. At the same time the eerie feeling returned, together with what I might describe as a sense of some impending horror that sent cold shivers down my spine. My scalp felt as though it was being loosened and my teeth chattered with cold. I sat there petrified, utterly unable to move hand or foot, in expectant terror.

How long this lasted I could not say; but presently I saw something move just outside the opening in the veranda wall, where the stench was coming from and where I had scattered the dry sand.

The first thing I saw was what I took to be the head of a very old native. Then the rest of the body appeared, crawling very slowly on hands and knees and not making a sound. Presently the creature came within the radius of the lamplight so that I could see it more clearly. A more horrible sight I have never seen, a more loathsome thing I hope never to see. The face was mottled with pock marks and the nose had been eaten away. The head was bald, the top of it being a dirty white, while the rest of the body was like old and mouldy leather, shrivelled and grey in patches. And the eyes—oh, those dreadful eyes. Never shall I forget them, as the head turned towards me. They were without life or expression, just two staring, dead eyes that did not move. The horrible, lipless mouth was half open, the jaw sagging like that of a dead person.

Slowly and silently it crawled across the sanded veranda. It was quite naked, and in one hand appeared to be holding a native-made rope, which it dragged after it as it moved.

It took not the slightest notice of me, nor of the lamp, nor of anything else; and presently it arrived within three paces of where I sat—frozen with horror and half stifled by the stench. I tried to call out, but my throat was paralysed and my lips refused to move. Every feature of the horrible thing was now clearly visible, and they were those of a partly decomposed corpse.

To add to my horror the light of the lamp seemed to grow dimmer and I feared it would go out, leaving me in the darkness in close proximity to this loathsome object.

Then, dimly, I saw it slowly rise to its feet, until it stood upright, facing me. It could not have been more than four feet six inches in height, and now showed all its naked foulness. The figure was that of a very old, shrivelled-up, decaying native; and it held the short piece of rope in its hand. Slowly it lifted up its arms, gripped the wall plate of the veranda, and started to climb the upright post supporting the roof.

Just as its feet left the ground the power to move came back to me, and I felt alive again. I raised my revolver and shouted 'Guzu!' (Ibo for stop, or halt). It took no notice. Again I called out 'Guzu!' Still it took no notice.

Then I fired two shots in rapid succession at point-blank range, expecting to see the body fall. But nothing happened. The creature continued to climb, eventually reaching the rafters, trailing the rope behind, but making absolutely no sound.

I then stood up, reached out until the muzzle of the revolver was only three or four feet from the mark, and fired again. Still nothing happened, and the figure continued to climb.

I knew then that it could not be human. My shots had gone through it, and it was unharmed, not a drop of blood having fallen to the floor.

I fled, not by the opening through which the apparition had come, but through another one at the end of the veranda near my bed. Then I yelled for my boys, for the police, for anybody, at the same time firing my revolver twice into the air to rouse them.

This caused considerable commotion in the lines, and there was much shouting and waving of lighted sticks as hurricane lamps were hastily ignited. But even then none of the members of my retinue were in any hurry to come in my direction.

However, they came at last—in a body—after much cursing and threatening on my part. They carried lamps and torches, and looked so scared that the least thing would have made them fly, panic-stricken, for their lives.

I ordered a lance-corporal of police to have the house surrounded, but not to enter it, telling him that a thief had climbed the roof and was still there. I instructed him also that anyone attempting to escape was to be arrested at once. Then, accompanied by two of my servants carrying lamps and matchets, I entered the house from the back, as I did not wish to disturb my 'sand traps'.

We searched the house without finding anything, and I noticed that the putrid smell was no longer perceptible. Then I carefully examined the places over which I had spread the sand. There was not a track!—not a mark of any kind!

There were two holes in the veranda post made by the two bullets from my revolver, one above another. And from their position the bullets must have passed right through the body of the 'thing' as it climbed the post.

There was also a bullet mark on the rafter along which it was crawling when I fired the third shot. It also showed that the bullet must have reached its mark.

It was gratifying to know that I had hit what I had aimed at—though even a poor shot with a revolver would have found it difficult to miss an object of that size at so short a range, and I was by no means a poor shot. But this proof made the whole thing more mysterious than ever. What was it I had seen? A ghost? The idea seemed absurd, because whatever it was, it had appeared to be solid enough. And the smell? I had never heard of a ghost that stank as this one had done.

There was but little sleep for any of the party during the remainder of the night. I sat in my deck chair and listened to the welcome sound of my people's voices as they discussed the occurrence. The voices were human, and therefore a comfort after what I had gone through, so I did not order silence as I would ordinarily have done.

When daylight came I had another thorough search made, again with negative results. Not a trace of anything was found, and the air was perfectly sweet and fresh once more.

I was determined to find out what I could about the history of the place. But I knew it would be of no use sending for the chiefs; they would, like all primitive peoples, tell as little as possible to a white man. So I sent the interpreter to the town with orders to find, if he could, an intelligent native.

After a while he returned with a bright-looking youth, dressed in khaki shorts and shirt, who informed me in moderately good English that his name was Benjamin Oku, and that he was a native of Isuingu, but had been educated at the Calabar mission, and was a clerk employed by one of the trading firms at Calabar. At present, he said, he was on leave, and was visiting his people, whom he had not seen since he was very young.

I did not tell him what I had seen the night before, but simply promised him a dash (i.e. a present or tip) if he could tell me the history of the rest house. Nothing loth, he agreed; and this is his story.

Long before the white man came to the place the ground on which the rest house had been built was the Ju-ju sacrificial grove. It was then bush, in the midst of which had stood a large cotton tree.

Hundreds of people had been sacrificed there, the Ju-ju being a very bad one, and its chief priest a very, *very* bad man.

At this point of the story Benjamin was at great pains to inform me that, of course, he had never had anything to do with the

A witch-doctor during a ceremonial dance.

sacrifices, indeed he had never even seen one, as he had been much too young to participate in such affairs when he was taken away by the missionaries. I let that pass and told him to proceed.

This Ju-ju priest, he continued, was greatly feared by the people of this and other towns for many miles around, as he was not at all particular as to the place from which he drew his victims, consequently none knew the day when they might find themselves 'smelled out' for sacrifice.

About two years before my visit troops had 'halted' for some weeks at Isuingu, and the white man in command had ordered the people to build a rest house, choosing as the site the Ju-ju ground. And although the chiefs and various others of the people had suggested other and better sites, he had been adamant— doubtless thinking this the best way to stamp out entirely the superstitious and savage customs the place stood for.

The old Ju-ju priest had evidently become crazy when he saw what was happening to his preserves, and lodged a violent protest. But the white man's reply to this had been to make him assist at the demolition of the grove. The same evening he had cast spells—cursing the place, and swearing that no white man should ever rest in peace in the house that was to be built on what, to him, was sacred ground. The chiefs and people had been terrified at these curses, but in spite of this they were obliged to build the house, and on the day it was finished the troops departed.

On the day after that the old priest was seen wandering round the house, repeating his spells and wailing loudly. The following morning his dead body was seen hanging from the main ridge-pole of the house, in the passage between the two rooms. He had evidently climbed up from the inside of the roof, an extraordinary feat for such an old man, and hanged himself with a piece of native rope.

The people had been too frightened to cut the body down; so it had hung there until it rotted. Then it had fallen piece-meal to the ground and been 'cleaned up' by the scavenger pigs of the town, so that nothing remained.

After this no one would go near the rest house, and many people journeying home from their farms after dark had seen the old man, just as I had, dragging the rope on his way to do what had ended his life.

I asked Benjamin if he had ever seen the old priest. He replied that, as a child, he had often seen him; and described him as being very small, very old, his skin shrivelled, and his face so badly pitted that his nose had been eaten away. Also his bald head was white in patches owing, as rumour stated, to his having fallen into the fire when young.

This description tallied in every way with that of the apparition I had seen during the night; there could be no doubt about that. And it made me think a bit, I can tell you.

At Benjamin's request I promised I would not let the chiefs or any of the townspeople know that he had told me this history. But I was determined that no other white man should go through what I had; so I called the chiefs and told them that the house was dirty and stank; that I was going to burn it, and that they would have to build another on a site which I would select.

I watched the effect of my words as they were rendered into the vernacular by the interpreter. All of the chiefs showed approval, and all agreed with alacrity to do what I told them; asking me to choose the site at once, and making no objections when I chose the best one in the place.

Before leaving I fired the house of evil, and watched it burn until only a few charred uprights remained.

In course of time the new rest house was completed, and I have since slept peacefully in it on many occasions. The site of the old one is overgrown with bush—derelict, for no natives will go near it, although there are 'farms' all round it, so much does its reputation cling as a bad, *bad* place.

What was it I saw that night? An elemental? The earth-bound spirit of the old priest paying for the crimes he had committed during his life? And how to account for the horrible and indescribable stench that pervaded the house when the apparition was 'appearing'? I cannot.

Ju-ju and Justice in Nigeria,
by Frank Hives and Gascoine Lumley.

What *did* Frank Hives see that night? Was it 'the earth-bound spirit of the old priest paying for the crimes he had committed during his life'? Or do you believe, with Valentine Dyall, that there is a perfectly natural explanation?

PUPPETRY?

Most Ju-ju cults include in their rites the worship of idols fashioned from wood or straw and hideously painted. Some of these oversized 'dolls' are remarkably life-like, judging by specimens I have inspected in various museums.

One of the world's oldest forms of entertainment, found in the ancient cultures of widely separated races, is the puppet-theatre. There is, of course, no evidence that Nigerian tribes ever practised this art, but it seems a simple step from fashioning dolls to making them move about by pulling strings.

Mr Hives saw the 'apparition' by moonlight. At first it was a vague shape, apparently crawling along in the shadows. Later it appeared to drag itself upright and climb up into the rafters. It was never exposed to powerful light and Mr Hives could not bring himself to touch it.

Let us consider this description—the face 'mottled with pock-marks' . . . 'jaw sagging' . . . 'dead eyes that did not move'. It seems to me a fair picture of a huge doll made of cloth, hide, and possibly wood pulp.

The thing 'dragged behind it' a long piece of rope plaited in the native style. Could he be certain, taking into account the lighting conditions and the shock he was suffering, that the *rope* was not dragging the *thing*?—or at least connecting it in some way with the rafters?

My chief suspect is Benjamin Oku. Though outwardly educated and civilised, he clung secretly to the barbaric beliefs of his forefathers. A man of such contrasts could have organised an elaborate trick to avenge the 'insult' of the destroyed idols and the forced building of the rest-house on 'sacred ground'. He would find plenty of willing accomplices among the leaders of the banned secret society, and probably among the local chiefs.

Benjamin, we surmise, had visited one of the towns, and chanced to see a puppet show. This experience gives him the basic idea for the 'haunting': a life-sized doll controlled by thin ropes or wires from the resthouse's rafters—or even from the outside of the roof above the veranda, through narrow slits or holes between the logs or sections of matting. To increase the chances of success he finds some way of frightening Hives's cook and gun-bearer into co-operating with the Isuorgu. Native herbs are added to the white man's food to induce a slight fever, sweating, sleeplessness, nervousness, and 'abnormal coldness'.

With a fine sense of drama, Benjamin sets the stage by throwing a scare into the porters, and planting large quantities of decaying meat in the hollow to provide a 'corpsey' smell. Then he builds up tension gradually—by overthrowing the veranda furniture with hooks lowered on lines from the rafters!

By the time the 'ghost-doll' is introduced Hives is in a con-fused, nervous condition, befuddled through lack of sleep after days on the march—the ideal victim. Thoroughly shaken, he makes no effort to tackle the intruder, but merely blazes away at it with his revolver—an action which must have delighted Benjamin!

In the morning it only remains for Benjamin to concoct a yarn about the Ju-ju priest's suicide, and his aim is achieved: the resthouse is burnt down and the Isuorgu tribe's honour is restored.

In my view the Rope-Man of Isuingu was more rope than man!

Unsolved Mysteries, Valentine Dyall.

Was it only a puppet that Frank Hives saw that night, or has Valentine Dyall, having found a workable theory, adapted the facts of the case somewhat to make them fit in with it?

If African witch-doctors possess such extraordinary powers over the white man, why did they allow so many of their own people to be sold into slavery?

Can the white man ever fully understand the secrets of darkest Africa or South America?

Ghosts

A ghost is defined as the spirit of a dead person appearing to the living. Some ghosts are seen in colour while others are seen in monochrome. They can appear completely lifelike or be as transparent as a beam of light. Ghosts usually appear in the clothes of their own particular period and, in spite of structural changes to their old homes, many still follow their ancient walks, up staircases and along balconies now no longer there.

According to legend, ghosts cannot cross water and they will not speak unless first spoken to.

In spite of many experiments in the field of extra-sensory perception, we are still no nearer to discovering the truth about them. Do they exist in their own right or are they only a figment of the observer's imagination? In the words of Dr Johnson, 'All arguement is against it, but all belief is for it.' And indeed there is an impressive body of evidence which, if judged on its face value, presents a good case for their existence.

Perhaps the best known ghosts are those associated with one particular building. The Society for Psychical Research estimates that in Britain alone there are more than seven hundred places—factories, council houses, churchyards, public houses, barracks, theatres, castles (there are one hundred and fifty of these)—where 'supernatural events are still a mystery'. From among these seven hundred the *Weekend Telegraph* selected six and sent Vivian Craddock Williams and photographer John Marmaras to investigate.

SADLY AMONG THE TURNIP LANTERNS—
A STORY FOR HALLOWE'EN

SAWSTON HALL—A dawn escape and Bloody Mary's ghost.

Ancestral home of the Roman Catholic Huddleston family for five hundred years, Sawston Hall in Cambridgeshire is a noble Tudor house. It broods a little darkly, but it is lived in. The owner, Captain Huddleston, invites us to spend a night in the haunted room: the Tapestry Room. No one can sleep there undisturbed.

We walk slowly through the house looking at the old things: a portrait of Mary I in the Great Hall, a lock of her hair, pale and fragile, in the Gallery.

'In 1553, before she became Queen, Mary spent a night here in the Tapestry Room,' says Captain Huddleston. Mary had received a message from the Duke of Northumberland asking her to go to London to see her brother, the cypher-King Edward VI. 'Her brother, she knew, had been ill. What she did not know was that he was already dead, that Northumberland planned to imprison her as soon as she arrived. She hurried south, but at Hoddesdon was warned that the message was a trap. She turned back and sought shelter for the night at Sawston Hall, home of John Huddleston, a papist.'

For Mary Tudor, the night in the Tapestry Room was short. Towards dawn, she was woken: a band of Northumberland's men was advancing on the house. Disguising herself as a milk-maid, she rode off in haste with a few friends. After a few miles they looked back on Sawston, and saw that the old house had been set on fire. 'Let it blaze,' she said. 'When I am Queen I will build Huddleston a finer house.'

So she did. The stones were taken from Cambridge Castle, and the house was finished in 1584. Little has changed since then. Dust settles. Everything sleeps. Mary should have left this house in peace, but did she?

Mrs Huddleston pulls the bell in the drawing-room to order dinner, her cook Mrs Fuller comes in, and our presence at Sawston is explained. The orders are given, but Mrs Fuller lingers at the door, her work-worn hands on the latch. She stares as us through her spectacles. 'I can tell you gentlemen there are ghosts here, most certainly. You have to be born on the chime of the hour to see spirits. I was born as the clock struck two.' I ask Mrs Fuller if she can describe any of the ghosts she has seen.

She nods. Most certainly. One of them was Queen Mary. 'She didn't say anything, she just drifted out. I could never spend a night here by myself—I just couldn't.'

At 7.30 p.m., dinner is served by candlelight. Our hosts are sceptical about the ghost in the Tapestry Room. 'If there is a ghost it is in the eye of the beholder.'

After dinner, we go upstairs. Captain and Mrs Huddleston retire to bed in another part of the house. The haunted room is dark, and hung with faded tapestries, the story of King Solomon. There are two doors, one in each corner, and against the wall a tall four-posted bed with a pale silk valance. We change for the night, and sit in armchairs by the door, John with his camera. It is very quiet, deathly quiet. When we speak, we speak in whispers. We are afraid of waking someone up. But there is no one in this part of the house.

11 p.m.: I lie on the bed to sleep. In the half-light, I see John slumped in his chair. It is very warm. I fall into a deep sleep. We are driving along the drive to the house. A woman tries to stop the car. She is distracted and pale. I drive on, though I want to stop. Then she appears again; the house is still a long way off. Her face is large and staring. There is a falling sound, as of an axe blade, a splash of blood. A woman's head lies in a basket, her eyes staring. A black hood grows larger and larger. It overwhelms me. I wake choking, in a sweat. John is shaking me by the shoulder. It is time to get up.

5 a.m.: I drink some water and look at the sky. The trees finger the edges of a cold dawn. I half expect to see figures running out from the woods. But everything sleeps.

I do not often dream. But the atmosphere of a house like this has a powerful effect.

FERRY BOAT INN—The wraith of a jilted girl.

Fenland's recorded history begins with Hereward the Wake hiding from the Normans in the reeds of the waterways criss-crossing this broad flat countryside.

In those times, between 1050 and 1100, near the reeds and the willow trees of the River Ouse there lived a girl who still lives on in a story told at the Ferry Boat Inn, on the edge of the river just beyond the village of Holywell in Huntingdonshire.

Her name was Juliet, a young girl who fell in love so deeply that it became with her a kind of illness. The man she loved was a woodcutter named Tom Zoul, a rough fellow who preferred a game of ninepins to the company of girls. Neglected by Tom,

Juliet pined away. A final sense of desolation overtook her on one of those ineffably sad days that you often get in the Fen country. She hanged herself on a tree by the river.

A frail girl in pink hanged on a willow by the River Ouse. The old women in the village shake their heads. There were no headlines in those days, but tongues wagged. The day was supposed to be March 17th.

Juliet had taken her own life; she could not be buried in the sanctified ground of a churchyard. Instead she was buried near the river and her grave was marked only with a plain slab of grey stone.

Many years later, the landlord who built the Ferry Boat Inn was short of stone—there are few quarries in the neighbourhood— so he built the floor of the inn around Juliet's gravestone. Juliet's grave is part of the inn's stone floor, and every visitor to the pub is shown it. On March 17th, for years, people have gathered late at the Ferry Boat Inn, to watch for Juliet's wraith to rise from the flagstone and drift out to the river.

In 1952, the landlord applied for a late-extension licence so that he could stay open legally for Juliet's night, and the evening was divided between drinking and story-telling. In 1954, four hundred people turned up at the pub and extra police had to come from near-by St Ives to control the crowd. In 1955, the Cambridge Psychical Research Society sent a team of investigators equipped with electronic detection apparatus to watch for Juliet's ghost. Not a shred of a wraith appeared; the men went home in a huff.

'Yet there have been some odd occurrences here,' says Mr Forrest, the present landlord, 'all of them very strange,' and he tells of a dog that would not go near the gravestone on any account, and of local women who will not go near the inn on March 17th.

This is a ghost that no one has ever seen, but which everyone talks about. It makes a point about apparitions. Ghosts will walk when love is not returned.

CLEVE COURT—The ghost who loves children.

Not far from the village of Minster in Kent there is a handsome red-brick early Georgian house called Cleve Court. In 1920, the lawyer and politician Sir Edward Carson was looking for a house when Cleve Court came up for sale. He and his wife liked it and bought it.

Sir Edward died in 1935, but until last August, Lady Carson lived at Cleve. Clear-sighted and practical, she was not, definitely not, given to flights of fancy. Yet she was convinced the house is haunted. Its ghost is a Grey Lady who has a habit of appearing when children are there.

'We had no idea we had bought a house with a ghost,' she told me when we called on her at Cleve. 'But soon afterwards, an old man in the village told me that a previous owner of the house, a long time ago, had been a tyrannical husband, who lived apart from his wife and kept her locked up. She died childless although she had wanted nothing more than children.

'At first my husband dismissed the story as a local romance. But it wasn't. Whenever there were children in the house, the Grey Lady appeared, and I have seen her myself.' That night John and I examined an elaborate bolt on the first floor, put there to imprison the Grey Lady in her room. The room led on to a landing, with tall windows overlooking the road. Even at dusk, Cleve Court seemed a pleasant house, bright and well-kept. But once, Lady Carson told me, she was saying good-night to one of her grandchildren 'when the girl pointed over my shoulder. "Who is she?" the girl asked. I looked round. Nobody was there.'

Another time: 'My great-niece asked her mother: 'Who is that nice lady we see at Cleve who nobody talks to?' Well, after a bit we knew who it was. The children were not in the least frightened.

'You see we like our ghost. She does no harm. I was furious the other day when someone suggested that we had her spirit laid.'

A benevolent ghost, pathetically seeking what she never found in life. A cogent story. But what actually was happening when Lady Carson saw the ghost herself? Was it real ectoplasm, with a physical presence? Or a vision?

Lady Carson smiled. 'I can only tell you what I saw. It was late at night. I let my spaniel out of the front door. I stood in the hall waiting for the dog to come back. Finally it came in. On the staircase it suddenly stopped in its tracks, and began whimpering and shivering. I looked up. On the landing was a grey lady floating down, noiselessly. I was so taken aback I couldn't say anything. She disappeared on the half-landing. I went into the drawing-room and sat down. It was definitely the Grey Lady.'

GLAMIS CASTLE—A family secret and, somewhere, a monster.

This is a fairy castle beyond compare. No other castle in Scotland has its chameleon-like power to change its character. In spring sunshine the old red stone glows and the turrets sparkle —a palace fit for a princess (in fact, Princess Margaret was born here in 1930). But in winter Glamis is very different. The swirling Scotch mist and driving rain transform it into a grey and ghastly shape. The castle becomes the castle of Macbeth, the shadows are thick with ghosts, and I challenge anyone to walk alone through the huge echoing rooms at night without fear.

No one knows how many rooms there are in Glamis. The Earl and the Countess of Strathmore live in a few at the back of the castle, their chauffeur-cum-butler in a flat overlooking the court-yard nearby. The Earl thinks there may be around a hundred rooms in all, but apart from their own, the others are deserted.

The huge reception rooms along the south front are still richly furnished, but not in use. In the summer they are open to the public, and so is the suite of rooms used by the Queen Mother when she stays in the autumn (the Queen Mother is a Bowes-Lyon, whose family seat Glamis is. The present Earl is her nephew). Above her suite is a maze of rooms—all empty and as cold as a morgue—where previous Earls used to accommodate their weekend shooting parties.

In this part of the castle alone I counted twenty-seven rooms. One of them was once occupied by Sir Walter Scott, who at the age of twenty spent a night at Glamis after a heavy dinner with the Earl's Factor. 'I must own,' he says in his *Letters on Demonology and Witchcraft*, 'that as I heard door after door shut after my conductor retired, I began to consider myself too far from the living and somewhat too near the dead.'

Late at night in this sinister place, it was easy to see what he meant.

The staircase that leads to these rooms is crowned with a clock tower. The clock still works, and its deep tick echoes eerily through the castle, sounding for the all the world like the heart-beat of a sleeping beast. At the bottom of the staircase is the core of the medieval castle, the long arched crypt, now lined with armour, swords, and other weapons of a savagery one rarely sees in England. Linked with it by dark staircases and a gloomy passage is Duncan's Hall, a small cramped cell which Shakespeare may have seen if, as some scholars believe, he visited Glamis on this way to Aberdeen with a troupe of players.

Glamis is the perfect setting for Macbeth, but there is no

record that King Duncan visited the castle or that he was murdered here. The only man known to have been murdered at Glamis is Malcom II of Scotland, in 1033. For years there was a bloodstain on the floor of the room called Malcom's Room. It may have been his, but there must have been many deaths here in medieval times, with wounded men coming in from battles to bleed unattended on the stone floors.

The walls in the old castle are immensely thick—up to fifteen feet in places. Somewhere in them lies the Secret of Glamis—a mysterious chamber where a previous Earl is supposed to have kept hidden a hideous monster, a son born half man, half beast.

For a hundred and fifty years this monster lived in the castle, only emerging to crawl about at night. The Secret, by custom of the family, is only known to the Earl and his heir. The present Earl says he was never told, though he is certain that the chamber exists, somewhere.

According to Lord Halifax, whose *Ghost Book* includes a chapter on Glamis, knowledge of the Secret had a profoundly depressing effect on all those who were told it. After a while the custom lapsed, though the mystery persists and the monster may still lurk in the walls.

Once in the 1880s, guests of the Bowes-Lyons made a concerted bid to locate the secret room. Their opportunity occurred when their host was called away to Edinburgh. From every room in the castle, they hung shirts and towels; then they gathered on the lawn outside to see if any window were unmarked. To their surprise they saw that there were seven. Before they could complete their search, their host's carriage reappeared and they were soundly rebuked for their curiosity.

One historical fact adds support to the legend. A portrait in the drawing-room shows the 1st Earl with his sons: two boys and a peculiar little dwarf.

BOSWORTH HALL—A damp blood-stain and Lady Lisgar.

Bosworth Hall at Husbands Bosworth in Leicestershire has been a Roman Catholic stronghold since 1630. Mrs Constable Maxwell's family have always lived there. Over time, the house has been changed a great deal. Stuart, Georgian, Victorian and modern additions give it an odd shape, full of rambling corridors and bent staircases.

Shortly after our arrival, Mrs Maxwell invites us to the chapel room, a low panelled room where Mass used to be celebrated by a resident priest before the Catholic church was built. On the pine floorboards underneath the sideboard we are shown a long dark stain. 'That stain is blood,' Mrs Maxwell says. 'It was spilled there three hundred years ago; it is still damp.'

A symbolic blood or wine stain—a relic of an interrupted Mass held here during the Cromwellian Protectorate. The priest was celebrating Mass, secretly—for Popery was outlawed and punishable by death. Suddenly, Cromwell's troops were heard riding up to the house. The priest leapt for the panelled door that led to his hiding place, a hole underneath the roof. As he leapt, he knocked over the chalice of consecrated wine.

'It is still damp,' Mrs Maxwell repeats, 'after all this time.'

I kneel and touch the stain. It *is* damp—a dark, waxy stain. I would like to scrape some up for chemical analysis. But you can't do that with other people's miracles.

The fire of Catholic faith still burns strong at Bosworth Hall. But there was another time when the practice of Roman Catholicism was rudely interrupted and equally the interruption had supernatural repercussions.

In 1881, Sir Francis Fortescue-Turvile, then head of the family, married a Lady Lisgar, a Protestant widow from Ulster, and, according to Mrs Maxwell, a haughty imperious woman. Lady Lisgar made extensive alterations to the Hall, all in heavy Victorian taste. None of this mattered in Catholic eyes, but when she refused to allow a priest into the house to give supreme unction to a dying maid-servant, she was damned forever to haunt the scene of her crime.

Mrs Maxwell describes the manifestations: 'I remember a doctor who saw Lady Lisgar's ghost when I was six. I was ill with typhoid. My parents had sought the Pope's intercession for my recovery. Until the benediction came, the family doctor was staying in the house in the room next to mine. On his way up from dinner one night he passed a strangely-dressed woman on the stairs. He said good-night but the woman did not answer. Next morning he asked my mother who the other guest was. "That is no guest" my mother answered. "That is the ghost of Lady Lisgar. I beg you not to mention it to the children."'

Whenever the pale spectre of Lady Lisgar is seen, drifting in the Bow Room where she slept and died, or floating at the end of passageways, Mrs Maxwell carefully records the event in the Black Book of Bosworth Hall. Every Easter, she has the rooms blessed by a priest.

One of the most recent entries in the book describes a canopy bed that Mrs Maxwell bought from a near-by lodge reputed to be riddled with poltergeist activity. From this bed one night not long ago, a guest was thrown with extraordinary force on to the floor.

Guests at the Hall once used to go to bed unwarned that there was some chance they would not sleep. At 4 a.m. they would awake to the most fearful creaks and groans. The ghost of Lady Lisgar? They lay sleepless until dawn dispersed the shadows and the eerie sounds subsided. Pale and shaking, they arrived at breakfast to be told by Mr Maxwell there was no cause for alarm.

The truth is that at 4 a.m. each morning the automatic central heating switches on. The warmth makes the old boards of the Hall expand, and the whole house creaks as though it were alive with ghosts.

BISHAM ABBEY—Blotted copy-books and Dame Hoby's ghost.

The Thames runs between low-lying meadows. We are at Bisham Abbey, near Marlowe, in Buckinghamshire. The rambling Tudor house stands on the edge of the river among trees, but as it is twilight it is not easy to tell its design. There is a chattering of voices, violating the silence. Since 1946, Bisham Abbey has belonged to the Central Council of Physical Recreation. The Council's students gather in the old hall for supper after their afternoon of sport.

From the walls, severe Tudor faces stare over the babble, and from the gallery hang flags, cobweb-thin with age, parts of which float down occasionally into the soup. Roars of laughter from the benches.

Miss Dickinson, who lives nearby, will tell you about the old house when the Vansittarts used to live here, and before. She will tell you how several students have been woken up in the dormitories at night by the sound of footsteps, shuffling along the corridor. But there is no corridor. And sometimes, by hysterical weeping. Was anyone crying last night? Of course not. The present generation have the time of their lives at Bisham. But years ago, people remember how two boys came back late one evening from fishing. They walked along the river bank in the twilight and saw among the shreds of mist on the water an old woman cowled in black sitting in a boat, somewhere between the Abbey and the church. They were afraid ever again to walk in the shadow under the trees.

Everybody knew it was Dame Hoby.

Dame Elizabeth Hoby died here in 1609 aged ninety-one and

lies buried in a fine tomb she had built for herself in Bisham church. But she died an unsettled spirit. Dame Hoby was guilty, it seems, of the death of her small son.

Her portrait in the Abbey shows her in the black and white dress of a widow, a grave woman with dark hard eyes. She was a formidable character, similar in temper to her friend Queen Elizabeth. Like the Queen, Dame Hoby and her family had a reputation for scholarship. She took pains with the education of her children. Her eldest son Edward went from Eton to Trinity College, Oxford, and later was to become, like his father Sir Thomas Hoby, a successful diplomat. But another of her sons was not so bright. The boy was not good at his books. One day he made so many mistakes that Dame Hoby boxed his ears. She hit him so hard that he died.

Some say that she did not beat him, but locked him in a lobby to finish off his work. Then Dame Hoby was called away by a message from the Queen. She left without telling the servants. When she came back, her son was lying dead at his desk, tear-stains on the pages of his book.

Dame Hoby never recovered. She carried her remorse into old age and beyond the grave. There are no records. This is all hearsay, local folklore.

With her head-dress trailing behind her, she is seen, Miss Dickinson says, drifting around the Abbey. And as she walks, she washes and wipes her hands in a bowl that moves in front of her. In Miss Dickinson's scrapbook is a photograph of Dame Hoby on a staircase in the Abbey. The steps show through her dress. But there is better evidence than what may be just photomontage. Better evidence too than Admiral Vansittart's account of a late-night chess-game with his brother in the panelled room where Dame Hoby's portrait hangs. 'We had finished playing,' the Admiral said, 'and my brother had gone up to bed. I stood for some time with my back to the wall, turning the day over in my mind. Minutes passed. I suddenly realised the presence of someone standing behind me. I tore round. It was Dame Hoby. The frame on the wall was empty. Terrified, I fled the room.'

Fact or fiction? During some alterations to the Abbey in 1840, strange relics of Dame Hoby's grief came to light. Workmen found some children's copybooks between the joists of the floor. One was badly blotted. When the books were asked for, they had been taken out of the house—sold, Miss Dickinson assumes, by the workmen. They have never been traced.

Article in *Weekend Telegraph*, by Vivian Craddock Williams.

Waiting for ghosts. These present-day Spiritualists meet weekly in a flat in North London. They are a 'home circle'—typical of hundreds all over the country. The circle is seen as completing a link between the members and the spirit world.

There are many people who profess to have seen a ghost. Have you ever seen one? Or have you friends or relatives who have?

Another type of haunting is carried on by ghosts who have unfinished work to be done. They are the ghosts of people who were executed for crimes they did not commit and return from the grave to clear their names or who come back to ensure that a friend or relative is not done out of his rightful inheritance or to tell of buried treasure. But by far the strangest case of a ghost with a purpose is the one which appeared to Gordon Collier at the end of the Second World War. The 'bizarre, unnerving' story of the . . .

FOUR FINGERS

In April of 1945, American Armed Forces launched an all-out attack to drive the Japanese from Cebu City, the second largest city in the Philippine Islands. By June, the Japanese were driven well beyond the city and mop-up operations were under way.

While Cebu City was being repaired and rebuilt to serve as an important supply depot for the invasion of the Japanese mainland, many of us who had taken part in the invasion were given opportunities of our own to repair the personal damages of jungle warfare. For some, this meant treatment for malaria and jungle rot. For me, it meant an infection of the middle ear that resisted all attempts at curing by the Army medics. They were without the necessary equipment.

By chance, I noticed an M.D.'s shingle on one of the few remaining houses in Cebu City that had withstood our bombing and artillery fire. The doctor was Max Borromeo. Because of him, my infection was quickly cured . . . and I was then exposed to one of the most bizarre, unnerving experiences of my life. 'There is no doubt about it,' the round-faced, gentle doctor told me after it was over. 'I have saved you from deafness in one ear. But you have saved me from death by slow, torturous exhaustion . . . or at the very least, from complete insanity.'

After my infection had been cured, I accepted an invitation to dine with Max Borromeo and his attractive German wife. Throughout the meal, I watched them exchange glances . . . of mutual love and mutual horror.

We were sitting over a glass of wine, when the conversation took a turn which produced a remarkable effect upon my host and hostess. I cannot recall what it was that started the topic of the supernatural, but it ended in my telling them of the many mediums and psychics I had visited. I concluded by narrating my experience at a materialisation seance at Casadega, Florida, where a number of spirits had appeared in a dark room, then became fully visible. One had a Confederate uniform with sword, epaulettes, complete.

My adventure was not exciting but it appeared to excite my listeners to the highest degree. The doctor's wife left the room and we smoked for a while in silence. I felt that his nerves were vibrating like fiddle strings. My instincts told me that he was on the verge of some intimate confidence, and I feared to speak lest I should interrupt it. At last, he turned towards me with the gesture of a man who has nothing left to lose.

'From what you have said, it seems to me that you are the very person I need. Being a veteran of jungle warfare, you must be cool and steady. I am not trying to flatter you. You have a knowledge of the occult and supernatural which may be brought to bear on the subject I want to discuss. As you have already seen some materialised "ghosts", an apparition would probably not scare you?'

'I think not.'

'As a student of the occult you would probably even be interested in investigating it?'

'Of course.'

'Believe me, there was a time when I would have said the same. My nerve was a by-word. And now you see me—one of the most timid and nervous persons in town. Do not feel too brave, or you may find yourself in the same boat as I am in—ready for the madhouse or the grave.'

After a silence, he continued: 'For some years, my life and that of my wife have been made miserable by a cause which is so grotesque that it borders on the ludicrous. And yet familiarity has never made it more easy to bear. As time passes my nerves become more worn and shattered by this constant wearing away. If you have no physical fears, I would value your opinion upon this phenomenon.'

'What is the nature of the phenomenon?' I asked.

'I think in order that you do not pre-judge the situation, I shouldn't tell you in advance what you may expect to encounter.'

He led me out of the dining-room and down a passage until we came to a large, bare room fitted as a laboratory. A shelf ran along one side upon which there stood a long line of glass jars containing pathological and anatomical specimens.

'These jars are the remains of a most excellent collection, but unfortunately I lost the greater part of them when my house and hospital were burned down by the Japs. I had examples of many rare conditions. These are the survivors.

'There is, as you see, a small settee here,' said my host.

'Since you are off duty tonight, it would be a great kindness on your part if you would consent to spend the night in this room. Please let me know if you don't feel like doing it. My room is next door, so if you want company, I will answer your call. I am a light sleeper.'

I cannot say I was looking forward to this night's sojourn. I have no more courage than the next one, but being somewhat familiar with spiritualism, I would not have the terror of the unseen that an average person might have.

I was sound and healthy, and so it was with the thrill of a sportsman who waits for his game that I shut the laboratory door behind me.

It was not an ideal atmosphere for a bedroom. The air was heavy with chemical odours, formaldehyde predominating. The odious line of glass jars with their relics of disease and suffering stretched in front of my eyes. An absolute silence reigned throughout the house, so that the low swish of the branches in the garden came softly and soothingly to my ears. It may have been the hypnotic lullaby of the murmuring of the trees, but in spite of my efforts to stay awake, I fell at last into a deep and dreamless sleep.

I was awakened by a sound in the room, and I instantly raised myself. At first I could see nothing; presently, as my eyes became accustomed to the faint light, I was aware, with a thrill that made my spine crawl up my back, that something was moving along the line of the wall. A gentle creaking of the floor came to my ears, and I dimly saw a human figure walking stealthily from the direction of the door. As it emerged into a patch of moonlight, I saw very clearly that it was a man. He appeared to be a native Filipino. He walked slowly, and his eyes were cast upwards towards the line of bottles which contained those gruesome remnants of humanity. He seemed to examine each jar with attention and then pass on to the next. When he had come to the end of the line, he stopped, faced me, threw up his hands with a gesture of despair, and vanished from my sight.

As he threw up his hands, I observed a singular peculiarity. Four fingers were missing from his left hand! In every other way his appearance was natural. I had seen and heard him so clearly that I could easily have believed he was a native servant of Dr. Borromeo's who had come into my room in search of something. It was only his sudden disappearance that suggested anything more sinister to me. I sprang from my couch, turned on the light, and examined the whole room carefully. There were no signs of my visitor, and I was forced to conclude there had really been something outside the normal laws of Nature in his appearance. I lay awake for the remainder of the night, but nothing else occurred to disturb me.

I am an early riser, but Dr Max was an even earlier one, for I found him pacing up and down the front porch.

'Well!' he cried. 'Did you see him?'

'Yes, I saw him.' I told him all that occurred. When I had finished, he led the way into his study.

'Before you return to your base, I want to give you a little explanation of this fantastic affair,' he said. 'In the first place when I tell you that for three years I have never passed one single night without my sleep being broken by this fellow, you will understand why it is that I am a wreck of my former self. His ritual is always the same. He appears by my bedside, shakes me roughly by the shoulder, passes from my room into the laboratory, walks slowly along the line of bottles, and then vanishes. For a thousand times he has gone through the same routine.'

'What does he want?'

'He wants his fingers.'

Dr Borromeo continued. 'After the invasion in 1942, we fled to the hills but some were not fortunate enough to get out of the city in time. As months passed by, some of these managed to escape and told stories of unbelievable cruelty. Jap soldiers would toss babies in the air and catch them on their bayonets. One man had been multilated capriciously by a Japanese soldier who had cut four fingers from his hand. The poor native carried the severed fingers with him and asked me to sew up the wounds. When I finished the sewing, the native asked what my fee was. I knew the fee was a matter of pride, so I told him his fee could be the fingers, which I would add to the remains of my collection I'd carried to the hills.

'He violently opposed the suggestion.

'According to his religion it was an all-important matter that the body should be reunited after death and so make a perfect dwelling for the spirit. Since his fingers were already off, I asked how he intended to preserve them. He said he would pickle them in salt and carry them with him. I suggested that they might be safer in my keeping than in his. Besides I had some formaldehyde to preserve them in. Realising that I really intended to preserve them, his opposition instantly vanished. "But remember, Doctor, I shall want them back when I am dead." I laughed at the remark, and the matter ended.

'A month later, a Jap patrol found our hideout in the hills and burned our houses. My wife and I were lucky to escape. My pathological collection was largely destroyed. What you see are the remains I recovered after the Japs were driven into the interior. The fingers of the native were burned and the unfortunate native himself was caught and killed by the Japs.

'Shortly afterwards I was awakened one night by a furious tugging at my sleeve. I sat up and I saw my patient. He was holding up his hand and looking reproachfully at me. I realised he was dead and that he had come to claim my promise of keeping his fingers for him. Every night at the same hour for three years this performance has been repeated. It is a simple ritual, but it has worn me out like water dripping on a stone. It has brought sleeplessness with it, for I cannot sleep now for the expectation of his coming.'

A week later, I had another night off watch and stopped by to see my doctor friend. To his surprise, I asked his permission to spend another night in his laboratory. The doctor was curious to know what I was going to do, but my fears of raising false hopes prevented me from telling him.

A book I had read on earthbound spirits claimed that a dominant idea possessing a spirit at the hour of death is sufficient to hold it to this world. Spirits are the amphibia of this life and of the next, capable of passing from one to the other as the turtle passes from land to water. The causes which may bind a soul so strongly to a life are any violent emotion. Avarice, revenge, anxiety, love, and pity—have all been known to have this effect of keeping a spirit bound to this world. It springs from some unfulfilled wish, and when the wish has been fulfilled the material bond relaxes. There are many cases on record which show the singular persistence of these spiritual visitors, and also their disappearance when their wishes have been fulfilled, or in some cases when a reasonable compromise has been affected.

No actual atonement could be made here—but a reasonable compromise! As soon as I had finished my watch, I made my way to a mortician. Without explaining why, I asked for the fingers from a native's hand.

'A dead man's fingers!' the mortician exclaimed in amazement.

After I put a five pesos note into his hand, he retreated into his embalming room. Presently he returned with a small package which he gave me.

I spent that night in the laboratory and I placed the package in one of the glass jars.

Sleep was out of the question. I sat with a shaded lamp beside me and waited patiently for my visitor. This time I saw him clearly.

He appeared beside the door, nebulous for an instant, and then hardening into as distinct a form as any living man. Again, he passed slowly along the line of bottles until he paused before the one with the fingers. He reached up to it, his whole figure quivering with expectation, took it down, examined it eagerly, and then, face convulsed with fury and disappointment, he hurled it to the floor. A crash resounded through the house. The native disappeared. A moment later my door flew open and Dr Max rushed in.

'You are not hurt?' he cried.

'No—but deeply disappointed.'

He looked in astonishment at the pieces of glass and the fingers lying on the floor.

'Good Lord!' he cried. 'What is this?'

I told him of my idea and its wretched sequel. He listened intently, but shook his head.

'It was well thought of,' he said, 'but I fear that there is no such easy end to my sufferings. Now I insist on one thing. You shall never sleep in this room again. When I heard that crash, I was scared to death that something had happened to you.'

He allowed me to spend the remainder of the night where I was and I lay there worrying about the failure of my attempted solution to the problem. With the first light of morning there were the fingers still lying on the floor to remind me of my fiasco. I looked at them and then I rubbed my eyes in amazement! I jumped from my couch and looked again. There were only *three* fingers lying there!

On my next day off, I returned to the mortician. He swore he had given me all the fingers. One of them must have dropped out of the package. However, with a few more pesos in his hand, he was glad enough to amputate another finger for me from another cadaver. My next night off duty I returned to the doctor's place with the material for a fresh experiment.

Dr Max would not hear of my occupying the laboratory again. It offended his sense of hospitality, and he could not permit it. I left the fingers, as I had the other night, and occupied a bedroom in another portion of the house, some distance from the scene of my adventures.

In the dead of night my host burst into my room, a flashlight in his hand. He was enveloped in a loose dressing gown, and his appearance might certainly have seemed more formidable to a weak-nerved man than that of the native of the night before. But it was not his entrance alone which amazed me. He seemed suddenly younger by twenty years, his eyes were shining, and he waved his hands in triumph over his head.

'We have done it! We have succeeded!' he shouted. 'My dear boy, how can I ever in this world repay you?' He seized my hand and wrung it until it hurt.

'It was only an experiment—a forlorn hope,' I stammered.

'I'll be troubled no more,' Dr Borromeo said. 'What has passed is easily told. You know that at a certain hour this creature always comes to me. Tonight he arrived at the usual time, and aroused me with even more violence than is customary. His disappointment of the other night increased the bitterness of his anger against me. He glared angrily at me, then went on his usual round. But in a few minutes he returned to my chamber, *smiling*! I saw the gleam of his teeth through the dim light. When he waved good-bye, I could see *all his fingers were on his hand*. So he vanished, I believe, forever.'

Dr Max Borromeo's hopes were realised. He was never again disturbed by the visits of the restless native in search of his missing fingers. Dr Max and his wife spent a happy old age, unclouded by trouble. He died peacefully ten years later.

Strange Horizons, by Gordon Collier.

According to D. J. West in *Psychical Research Today*, it is 'the general rule that apparitions never leave behind physical traces of their visits. There are no footmarks and no displaced objects. This is one of the features that distinguishes these cases from ghosts in fiction.' And yet the ghost in this story hurled a bottle to the floor. Should this account then be taken literally?

Undoubtedly, many people who have seen ghosts have expected to see them. They have gone to a particular haunted spot, their minds conditioned by all they have read and heard. We often see what we expect to see.

As a schoolboy I used to practise on the organ in a twelfth century Norfolk church. It was a gloomy old building surrounded by a large graveyard and my mind often dwelt upon thoughts of ghosts and the supernatural. One evening, having mastered one of the simpler Bach preludes and fugues, I switched off the organ light and made my way down to the nave. As I did so a sinister figure in a black cloak materialised from one of the pews and came slowly towards me. Fear held me motionless. Then I saw the cause of my dread. My phantom was nothing more than the shadows thrown up by a street lamp playing upon one of the pew ends. In the same way, Sir Walter Scott was convinced that he had seen the ghost of the poet Byron at his home at Abbotsford—until it was pointed out to him that in the uncertain light he had mistaken clothing hanging on a peg in the hall for the poet's ghost.

This splendidly ghostly photograph from the archives of the Society for Psychical Research shows what can be done with a darkroom, some basic photographic techniques and lots of imagination!

Sometimes an unexpected happening can give rise to a ghostly tale. A vicar of Redruth in Cornwall was out for a stroll during the latter part of the eighteenth century when he saw a diabolical monster breathing flames and smoke coming towards him. He fled in terror. Later he discovered his 'dragon' was an early steam engine driven by James Watt's foreman, William.*

Many ghost stories later turn out to be hoaxes. Or they may be the product of a vivid imagination, such as the Angel of Mons who was supposed to have appeared in the sky to prevent the Germans from taking advantage of the British defeat. The story was later found to have been a complete fabrication written by an over-imaginative journalist.* Or maybe they are hallucinations. Consider, for example, the case of . . .

THE PHANTOM FLYER

Lieutenant David McConnell was a British trainee pilot in the First World War. He was eighteen, and just about to receive his 'wings', when the tragedy took place. On the morning of December 7th 1918 he was unexpectedly asked by his Commanding Officer at Scampton to fly a 'Camel' aircraft to Tadcaster, a distance of sixty miles. At 11.30 a.m., McConnell took leave of his room-mate Lieutenant Larkin, saying that he had to take an aeroplane to Tadcaster instead of going to machine-gun practice, but that he expected to be back for tea. Another pilot, in a separate two-seater machine, accompanied McConnell with the intention of bringing him back to Scampton after the 'Camel' had been delivered. The weather was fair when they set out, but at Doncaster they ran into fog, and came down to telephone for instructions. McConnell was told to use his own discretion, so they took off again. The fog got thicker and McConnell's companion made a forced landing. McConnell, continuing, reached Tadcaster, but nose-dived and crashed on his way in. He was thrown violently forward, his head smashing into the gun in front of him. A young woman who was watching ran to the spot and found him dead. His watch had stopped at exactly 3.25 p.m.

At the funeral, which was held four days later, David McConnell's father was told by Lieutenant Hillman, another member of the unit, that, at the moment of the crash, David's apparition was supposed to have been seen by his room-mate Lieutenant Larkin. The father wrote to Larkin almost immediately. In his reply, dated December 22, Larkin set down a clear account of his experience. On the afternoon of McConnell's flight to Tadcaster, he was sitting in front of the fire reading and

* *The Realms of Ghosts*, by Eric Maple.

smoking. He heard footsteps coming up the corridor, and then the familiar noise and clatter that McConnell always made when he came in. Then he heard the greeting 'Hallo boy!' Larkin half-turned round to look towards the door, which was eight feet behind where he was sitting. There was McConnell standing in the doorway. He was smiling, and one hand was resting on the door-knob. He was dressed in flying kit, but wearing a naval cap in place of a flying helmet. This was customary with him as he was very proud of some experience he had had in the Royal Naval Air Service. Larkin remarked, 'Hello! Back already?' The supposed McConnell replied, 'Yes. Got there all right. Had a good trip.' Then, with a parting, 'Well, cheerio,' he went out and closed the door. Shortly afterwards, at a quarter to four, Lieutenant Garner Smith came into the room and said that he hoped McConnell would get back early enough for them to go out together that evening. Larkin said that McConnell was already back and had just been in the room. Larkin was sure that he saw the apparition somewhere between 3.15 and 3.30 p.m. Garner Smith confirms that it was 3.45 p.m. when he came into the room and Larkin told him he had just seen McConnell. The appearance of McConnell had been so ordinary and natural that Larkin thought nothing of it at the time. He heard news of the crash during the evening. At first he was so sure that it was McConnell in the flesh that he had seen, that he thought McConnell must have returned and then gone up again. Larkin remarks that he has no explanation to offer. He is sceptical on psychic matters, and would like to persuade himself that he never saw McConnell that afternoon, but he knows he did. Lieutenant Hillman confirms that on the morning after the crash Larkin told him the whole story exactly as related in the written version.

It is worth considering this case in detail, because it is a good example of a type of which there are many others on record. One cannot base any firm opinion upon a single case, and a long discussion of the pros and cons of a particular anecdote may seem trivial, but it is worthwhile because essentially similar considerations arise in the evaluation of all spontaneous cases. The McConnell case has several outstanding features. The coincidence in time between apparition and death is very close. The circumstances were recorded fairly soon after the event. The corroborative evidence of Lieutenant Garner Smith shows that Larkin described the apparition before he could possibly have known about the crash. Larkin's testimony is set down in an orderly, sober manner that is most persuasive, but as with all such anecdotes there are loopholes apparent to the really sceptical.

One possible explanation on normal grounds is that some other flyer looked into the room where Larkin was, and that Larkin mistook him for McConnell. This is not a plausible explanation when one considers the distinctive feature of McConnell's naval cap, which Larkin specially noted. Even if it were a case of mistaken identity, it would still be a remarkable coincidence that such an extraordinary mistake, in itself amounting practically to a hallucination, should occur just at the time of McConnell's accident. The incident would be less striking if Larkin had been dozing and had merely dreamed about McConnell. Dreams are so frequent and so varied that chance alone can bring about most striking coincidences. However, Larkin is clear that he was awake and smoking at the time. It would be easier for the sceptic to deny the whole story. Perhaps Larkin was lying. Perhaps he had some reason for telling Garner Smith he had seen McConnell. Perhaps both Garner Smith and Larkin were lying. It may be they invented the story to comfort McConnell's parents; or perhaps it was just devilment. If both Larkin and Garner Smith had been subjected independently to expert questioning immediately after the alleged experience, maybe some flaw would have been discovered. As it was, the written statements were forwarded to the late Sir Oliver Lodge and published without mention of further investigation. It is the besetting sin of the true sceptic to imagine that, if only *he* had been on the spot, something might have been found that would have changed the whole complexion of the case.

Deliberate lying can account for few of the cases published by the London or American Society for Psychical Research, otherwise one would hear more of the boastings of those who had successfully hoaxed the investigators. Of course there have been hoaxes, but mostly the hoaxers get discouraged when they realise how much information the investigators demand.

Returning to the McConnell case, what other explanations are there apart from lying? The most naïve theory is that it was McConnell's ghost that Larkin saw, a quasi-physical phantom that was sufficiently tangible to open the door and make a noise. Now it will be remembered that the apparition was said to have closed the door after it, thus leaving things as they were before it appeared. This is in line with the general rule that apparitions never leave behind physical traces of their visits. There are no footmarks and no displaced objects. This is one of the features that distinguishes these cases from ghosts in fiction. We know by analogy with many similar experiences that, if a second person had been present, it is unlikely that he would have either seen or heard McConnell's apparition. The McConnell apparition was unusual in being so very life-like, and in being talked with as well as seen. In most cases the apparition is seen as a mute figure, often misty and unreal. Sometimes an apparition is not 'seen' at all, but felt as a 'presence'. Apparitions are not physical phantoms that can be photographed. They are subjective and, in the strict sense, hallucinations.

It is almost certain that, if genuine, Larkin's experience was a hallucination. The question at issue is not how the hallucination occurred—that is a psychological problem—but why it occurred just at the moment McConnell was killed. What is the connection, if any, between McConnell's death and Larkin's experience? The theory favoured by most investigators is that Larkin became aware, subconsciously, and by means of ESP, that McConnell had been killed, and that this subconscious knowledge, striving to gain expression, gave rise to the hallucination. Are there any other theories that do not involve ESP?*

None of the explanations in normal terms is satisfactory, but one of the least implausible is that Larkin's hallucination was induced by an expectant state of mind. There is no doubt that expectancy sometimes produces hallucinations. Psychologists who have studied illusions have demonstrated that in ordinary perception we are apt to see, not what is actually present, but what we think is there. If an appearance is suggestive of something familiar, the observer unconsciously projects on to the field of view his own preconceptions, and sees the objects he knows rather than the real thing. This unwitting falsification is most evident when the observer's emotions are aroused by something he is expecting or hoping to see. It is a common experience, when waiting for a friend, to recognise him approaching in the distance, only to be disappointed when at close quarters he turns out to be a stranger. Another example, of which I happen to have heard two cases, is that of a person who turns on the radio, and sees the dial light up as expected, when all the time the current was switched off. Society for Psychical Research investigators have collected a number of cases in which apparitions—that is to say hallucinations of realistic human forms—appeared as a result of expectancy. The case of Mrs T. E. is an example. She was sitting in a hotel room waiting for her husband when she clearly saw him approaching and got up to meet him. The figure vanished before her eyes.

In the McConnell case, Larkin was expecting his friend to

* Extra-Sensory Perception: the ability to acquire knowledge without using the normal senses.

return around tea-time. If news of the fog had reached Scampton, he may have been a little anxious. A condition of anxious expectancy is just that state of mind most likely to induce a hallucination in persons inclined to have these experiences. The weak point in this explanation is that Larkin stated that the experience *was* for him quite exceptional. There is no doubt that had he been questioned on the point he would have rigorously denied that he was subject to hallucinations, expectant or otherwise. The coincidence remains. Larkin had a most unusual experience just at the time his friend was killed. Could it have been a chance coincidence?

The plausibility of chance coincidence as an explanation depends upon the frequency of hallucinations in sane and wakeful persons. If hallucinations are common, as dreams are common, then an occasional coincidence with a real event would not be so extraordinary. Now hallucinations are really only waking dreams, just as dreams are hallucinations during sleep. It is well known that there is a repressive mechanism that causes dreams to be quickly forgotten. The man who says 'I never dream' is able to remember his dreams if questioned immediately on waking. Is there a similar repressive mechanism that would make someone like Larkin declare that he never had hallucinations when in fact he did have them? Both propositions have been shown to be true. Hallucinations are much commoner than is generally supposed, but there is a marked tendency to forget very quickly ever having experienced them. The investigations of these points are so interesting and important that we must digress from the discussion of the McConnell case in order to describe them.

It is to the Census of Hallucinations carried out in 1890 by a Society for Psychical Research committee, and published in a four hundred-page report, that we owe our information about the frequency of hallucinations in normal persons. The investigators sent round representatives to explain what was wanted and to obtain answers to the following question: 'Have you ever, when believing yourself to be completely awake, had a vivid impression of seeing or being touched by a living being or an inanimate object, or of hearing a voice, which impression, so far as you could distinguish, was not due to any external physical cause?'

The total number of answers received was 17,000, of which 2,272 were in the affirmative. The investigators were not convinced that all those who answered 'yes' had had real waking hallucinations. Some of the positive replies referred to dreams, to half-waking experiences, to the hearing of footsteps or odd sounds, to images conjured with closed eyes, or to vague feelings of a 'presence'. When all these were excluded, there remained 1,684 positive replies. That is to say, nearly 10 per cent of the 17,000 persons questioned admitted to having had at least one definite hallucination that could not be attributed to illness or intoxication. Fifty-eight years later I sent out the same question through Mass Observation, an organisation which has conducted many questionnaire investigations. This time, a rather higher proportion, 14 per cent of the 1,519 replies received reported definite hallucinations. There was, anyhow, no suggestion that hallucinations are becoming less frequent.

The Census investigators were well aware of two sources of error. Some who had had experiences may have refrained from answering in order to avoid embarrassment, and the interviewers may have had a tendency to select for questioning those of their acquaintance who would be likely to report experiences. To overcome both these errors the investigators questioned a number of compact groups, such as dinner parties and social gatherings, where everyone was prepared to answer, and there could be no unfair selection. Under these circumstances they got about the same proportion of positive answers. It is unlikely that deliberate untruthfulness accounted for many of the positive replies. It is more likely that some said 'no' when they should have said 'yes', because they did not want to make an admission which would invite more questions.

Most of the hallucinations were realistic human apparitions. There were 77 per cent of this type in the Census count, $79\frac{1}{2}$ per cent in the Mass Observation survey. Women reported hallucinations more often than men. In the Census returns there was an approximately equal number of men and women who sent in negative replies, but of those who answered 'yes', there were over half as many again of women as of men. In the Mass Observation survey more men than women answered 'no', but twice as many women as men answered 'yes'.

The figures show that hallucinations of human figures, like that of Lieutenant McConnell, are commoner than one would expect, but they still seem to be somewhat unusual. Of those who report such experiences, only a minority say they have had more than one in a lifetime. But there is the factor of forgetfulness to be considered. The Census also showed that there were over eight times as many hallucinations reported to have happened in the immediately preceding three months as in three-month periods nine or ten years back. Most of the hallucinations must have been forgotten. Those included in the Census count were the minority that some circumstances had caused to be remembered.

The Census investigators wanted to find out whether hallucinations of recognised human figures coincided with the death of the person 'seen' more often than could be accounted for by chance. They found sixty-five cases among their collection in which it was maintained that the apparition was seen within twelve hours before or after the death of the person concerned. This, they argued, was far beyond what could come about by pure chance. They even quoted death statistics to prove the point. The conclusion is scarcely surprising. The most resolute sceptic could not maintain that chance alone would account for all the cases of apparitions said to coincide with death. The Census investigators thought they had reduced the problem to a clear issue between chance coincidence and a psychic explanation. They had made what they considered were generous deductions to cover other explanations, like faulty reporting and the selective forgetting of non-coincidental cases. But the numbers they deducted were arbitrary. It is open to the sceptic to assert that the normal factors which the investigators admitted might account for a high proportion of the reported coincidences could just as well account for all of them.

The Census investigators quoted in full the twenty-six most evidential cases of death coincidences in their collection. None of these cases was really well corroborated; certainly none of them came anywhere near the standard of the McConnell case. What made this case so exceptional in evidential value was that it was written down fairly soon after the event. In most of the published cases the reports were not written until long after, when the stories had had time to become rounded off.

Psychical Research Today, from D. J. West.

What did Larkin see? Could another pilot have borrowed McConnell's naval cap and Larkin mistook him for McConnell? Could Larkin have dreamed that he was smoking as well as dreaming that he saw McConnell? Were Larkin and Garner Smith speaking the truth? Did they invent 'the story to comfort McConnell's parents'? Was it just a hoax, a piece of youthful devilment? Or did Larkin really see the ghost of Lieutenant David McConnell?

Or does the answer lie in telepathy? At the moment of death do some people send out a telepathic message to a friend or relative strong enough to create in the mind of the receiver a convincing picture of their physical presence?

If we stay in a house which is haunted, but are ourselves unaware of its supernatural connections, do we pick up telepathically from those around us their own thoughts and fears of the unknown rather

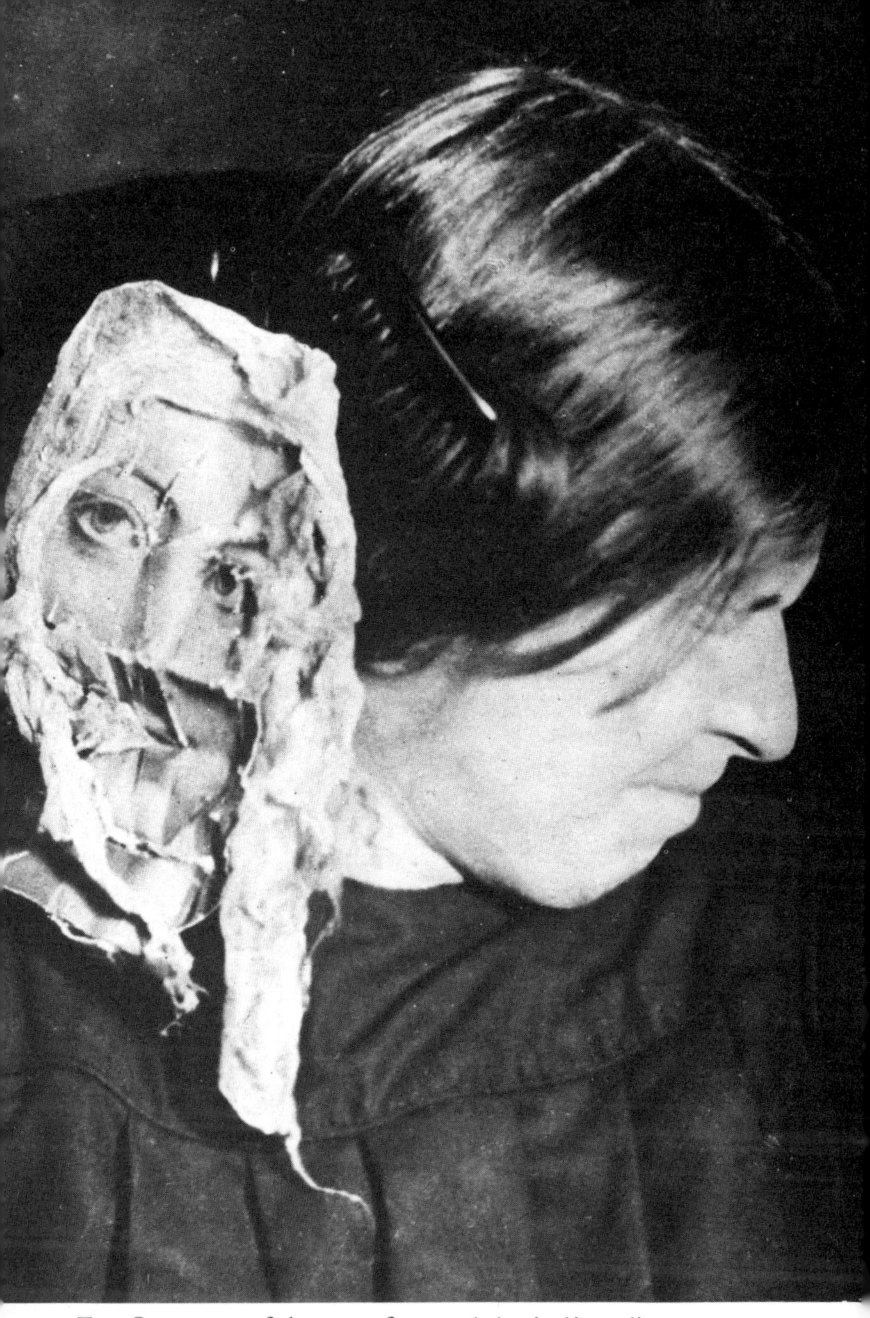

Eva C was one of the most famous 'physical' mediums in the Spiritualist heyday around the turn of the century. The 'spirit' face in the picture, taken in 1912, was probably made of pulpy paper, surrounded by veiling of some kind—you can just see the torn ends. But the atmosphere of a seance is highly emotional. If you want to see the face of a dead friend, that is what a crumpled newspaper will look like.

as a television set can pick up the signals sent out by an amateur radio enthusiast?

And, if not from other living persons, can telepathic messages from those now dead be stored, imprinted like a transfer on to walls or furniture, waiting to be picked up by those sensitive enough to receive them?*

Telepathy can be demonstrated under laboratory conditions, but no ghost has yet been materialised under strictly scientific conditions.

The most tragic type of ghost is surely the harbinger of death, the ghost who appears to foretell the death of a friend or relative, and when this happens on a large scale as it did in the village of Haidam in the summer of 1720, the events can be extremely horrifying. . . .

VILLAGE OF WALKING DEAD

A tall, splendidly garbed stranger rode into the courtyard of the University of Fribourg, Switzerland, one May morning in 1730, reined-up with a flourish and loudly demanded the way to the rector's office.

A group of students strolling under the portico turned curious eyes upon the rider. He had the lean, elegant features of an aristocrat, the proud yet easy bearing of a soldier. His voice was deep and cultured, but the accent foreign.

What could such a man want with the rector? This was no scholar—his very presence seemed to shatter the atmosphere of academic tranquility . . .

One of the students advanced and bowed politely.

'The rector is not here, sir. He is ill. But I will take you to the offices.' The stranger nodded and dismounted. The student stepped nearer and added, 'If you will tell me your name, and the nature of your business here . . . ?'

But the visitor was not to be drawn so easily.

'Just take me to the offices, lad,' he said curtly. 'I will explain myself there.'

The youngster flushed and, striving to ignore the soft laughter of his companions, led the way across the courtyard. Minutes later, after sharp exchanges with clerks and minor officials, the stranger was ushered into the office of the University librarian.

The small, elderly figure behind the huge desk in the middle of the room rose and greeted his anonymous caller in a mild, piping voice, 'I'm at your service, sir—whoever you are . . .'

The stranger hesitated, looking all about him—at the shelves packed tight with volumes of every size and description: at the

* *Ghosts and Hauntings*, by Dennis Bardens.

maps of remote, newly discovered lands which draped one wall, and the jumble of scientific papers that littered the librarian's desk. Then he drew himself up, bowed stiffly and said: 'I am the Count de Cadreras. My home is in Austria, but I am spending some time in your country, and I have heard that here a scholar's mind remains free and open—not ruled by church or state. Is this true?'

The old man stared for a moment, taken aback by the directness of the question. Then he nodded, 'Yes—it is quite true, Count.'

'Very well then!'

The Count strode to the desk, brushed books and papers to one side, dipped a quill in ink and handed it to the startled librarian.

'I have a story to tell—an amazing and terrible story, but a true one. I will give you the facts, and you can write them down. If they are properly recorded, perhaps one day men will find a natural explanation. . . .'

He spoke urgently, and with obvious sincerity. The old man took the pen and sat down without protest.

For the next two hours the only sounds in the room were the drone of that deep, guttural voice, the scratching of the quill— and an occasional horrified gasp from the librarian. . . .

The Count's story was set down exactly as it fell from his lips —in blunt, matter-of-fact phrases. The completed, signed manuscript was left in the University's keeping—but from that day to this no natural solution has been found to the grim problem it posed.

Through the intervening centuries the Cadreras manuscript has led many investigators to comb the museum archives of Austria and half a dozen other countries: a wealth of documentary evidence has been unearthed to corroborate, down to the smallest detail, the mystifying, terrifying tale of 'the village of walking dead'.

The facts are placed beyond all doubt by the number and rank of the witnesses supporting Cadreras—eminent lawyers and theologians, Austria's foremost surgeons and physicians, a host of distinguished army officers and various personal emissaries of the Emperor Charles VI.

Fraud is inconceivable: what could such a large and diversified company possibly hope to gain by confirming the weird reports of superstitious peasants and soldiery? Indeed, they had everything to lose by incurring the wrath of outraged religious leaders and an incredulous Emperor . . .

It is difficult to imagine how more reliable testimony is to be obtained of an event of the past. Working from translations of the original documents, and guided by the writings of the Rev. Montague Summers, the twentieth-century Englishman and prominent occult investigator who carried out meticulous research into the affair, I have built up this picture of the horror that threw a nation into panic and despair.

In 1720 the Austrian Empire of the Habsburgs was passing through a period of comparative calm after nearly two centuries of almost continuous wars—mainly with France and Turkey. Military chiefs were taking advantage of the lull—or 'cold war' period—to build up the army to full strength, ready for a renewal of fighting.

Joachin Hubner, a young man from Vienna, was one of many thousands of newly trained troops concentrated in the south-eastern provinces. In June he found himself billeted with a family of farming folk in the lonely village of Haidam, close to the Hungarian frontier.

Joachin thought himself lucky. In mid-summer the countryside was beautiful and duties were light. His billet was comfortable, the food was good, and he was treated as one of the family. He was a man of simple needs and easy contentment, and rural life suited him so well that he swore he never wanted to see the city again . . .

After dinner one evening, while the women of the household were at work in the kitchen, Joachin lingered at the table drinking wine and talking with his host and the farmer's fifteen-year-old son. It had been an exceptionally hot day, and now the main door had been opened wide to catch the cool breezes which sprang up with the dusk.

The host was telling a tale of his youth, laughing merrily, when suddenly a shadow fell across the table. Instantly the farmer stiffened, stopped in mid-sentence, and stared towards the door with glazed eyes. Joachin and the boy were sitting together with their backs to the door. Simultaneously they turned their heads to see who had entered.

Standing just inside the room was an old man. Untidy locks of snow-white hair surmounted a deeply wrinkled, rather vacant face. Large, watery eyes blinked at them and a gnarled hand was raised in customary greeting.

At first sight of the newcomer the boy stiffened as his father had done scant seconds before, and sat like one in a trance. Joachin was puzzled—the old fellow seemed a harmless figure. . . .

'What's the matter?' the soldier asked after a long silence. But he got no answer.

The old man shuffled forward to the table and lowered himself into a chair. The farmer and his son continued to stare fixedly at him, and Joachin noticed that both their faces held the same expression—one he had never seen before. At once he could read the signs of fear . . . amazement . . . and a deep, infinite sorrow . . .

For several minutes they sat in silence, the four of them.

From the kitchen there drifted the cheerful chatter and laughter of the women of the house, and the clatter of dishes. Somewhere outside a dog barked and a cart rumbled by. But in the main room nobody spoke and nobody moved.

At length Joachin, bewildered and embarrassed, tried to break the spell. Self-consciously he muttered a welcome and pushed the wine jug towards the old man.

The visitor did not seem to notice the gesture; he remained silent for fully a minute more, then suddenly stretched one hand across the table and touched the farmer's shoulder.

For the first time the host moved: he slumped forward, buried his face in his hands and drew a deep, heart-rending sigh. A moment later the old man got up and slowly walked out into the deepening twilight.

Joachin went to the door and watched him cross the road and disappear among the lengthening shadows in the village square. When he turned back the farmer had raised his head: great tears were rolling down his face.

'What ails you?' Joachin demanded. 'What does all this mean?'

But still no one answered him. The farmer got to his feet, stumbled across the floor and up the stairs to his bedroom. The boy watched him go, then suddenly gave a loud cry and rushed into the kitchen.

Joachin heard him talking excitedly, but the words were lost in a chorus of feminine shrieks and a crash of breaking crockery. Then all the womenfolk, wide-eyed and gasping, came hurrying across the room and, led by the excited youth, charged upstairs.

The young soldier stood at the bottom of the stairs, listening to a growing commotion—wails, moans, and sobbing. He started to climb the steps, but changed his mind: the cause of the alarm was probably some family problem, some intimate affair that was none of his business.

Having no wish to intrude, he shrugged off his curiosity and slipped away to spend the evening at the village inn. When he returned at midnight the house was in darkness and all was quiet: he went to bed and, heavy with wine, soon fell into a deep sleep.

In the morning he was awakened by the sound of women

crying. Hurrying from his room he almost collided with the farmer's son: the youth was carrying a wreath. . . .

'What has happened?' Joachin asked.

'My father is dead.' The boy's voice was flat and his expression was strangely listless.

Joachin was amazed—the farmer had been a robust, vigorous man in the prime of life.

'B— but how can that be . . . ? Only last night . . .' And then he broke off, remembering the peculiar episode he had witnessed. 'That old man—what had he to do with this?'

The lad regarded him in silence for several seconds, then answered in the same impressive tones, 'That old man was my grandfather—my father's father.'

'Yes . . . ? Well, I don't see what that has got to do with it!'

'No?' Into the boys eyes there crept a strange and dreadful light.

'*My grandfather has been dead and buried for ten years!*' he said.

Within the hour the fantastic tale had spread throughout the village and the surrounding countryside. Joachin told his comrades, and they repeated it to their officers and the families with whom they were billeted. The old man, it was said, had come back 'to summon his son to the grave . . .!'

Two days later an angry general ordered an official inquiry 'into this wicked rumour that causes such perturbance among the troops and citizens. . . .' To supervise the investigation he chose the commander of a corps of Alandetti Infantry—the Count de Cadreras.

Accompanied by an experienced army surgeon, a notary, and several other officers, the Count journeyed to Haidam and set up headquarters in the small church there. Joachin Hubner was interrogated throughout the whole of one day, then a sworn deposition was taken from each member of the dead man's household.

At the end of it all the investigators, deeply impressed, unanimously decided that the old man's body should be exhumed. Without delay they went out into the little churchyard. Before a silent crowd of villagers and troops, the coffin was taken up and opened. . . .

The army physician gave a startled cry as he bent over the body: the old man who had been buried ten years ago looked as though he had been dead for only a few hours. . . . !

The more nervous onlookers turned and hurried to their homes, and the others stood huddled together, some distance from the graveside, as the surgeon took a knife and pricked a vein in the corpse's arm. Warm, red blood trickled from the wound. . . .

'Incredible!' breathed the surgeon. 'He is dead . . . and yet alive!—as they say a vampire endures!'

'Then I suggest we deal with him as a vampire!' the Count said grimly. 'Drive a stake through the heart and strike the head from the body!'

The other investigators nodded: none of them believed in the existence of vampires—but there seemed nothing else to do. There could be no denying that somehow the old man's body had become reanimated—and they must take each and every precaution to ensure that it did not happen again. . . .

The gruesome operation was duly carried out and the corpse was laid back in its grave. The villagers and the soldiers sighed with relief—satisfied that it would rise no more.

The Count's report, countersigned by the other investigators, so startled the general that he forwarded it to the highest army tribunal. The tribunal, equally astounded, sent it to the Emperor.

A few weeks later Cadreras was ordered to present himself at court. For hours on end Charles VI sternly questioned him, going over every point of the story, plainly striving to trap him into some contradiction.

Failing to shake the Count's testimony, Charles ordered him to return to the village—accompanied by a Royal Commission. There was no mistaking the veiled threat: if the second investigation did not yield the same results, Cadreras and his colleagues would be punished.

The learned members of the Commission made no effort to conceal their scepticism during the journey to Haidam, and the Count must have wondered whether, at this late date, he would be able to convince them of the truth. But he need not have worried: waiting for them now was a mystery infinitely more terrifying than the first.

Entering the village they found many houses abandoned, others barred and shuttered: although it was broad daylight, the streets were empty: at the army post they found only the officers and a handful of men—the bulk of the troops had deserted. . . .

From those who still remained they heard a story of death and horror—a living nightmare that had driven whole families raving mad and sent villagers and soldiers fleeing in terror into the open country. . . .

Witness after witness—some half-crazed and gibbering with fear, others stunned and grief-stricken—attested on oath that they had been visited by long-dead relatives. . . . And on each occasion a villager had died within a few hours. . . .!

Haidam, they swore, was besieged by 'an army of corpses'! Each evening, as the sun began to set, the churchyard gave up its dead: all night long corpses stalked the streets, trying to get into the houses where they had once lived.

And when barred doors and windows denied them entrance, the ghastly invaders often cried aloud the names of their victims —with the same terrible effect. In all, the loathsome harbingers had taken twenty-one people, of all ages, back to the churchyard with them. . . .

The Commissioners did not wait for dusk to bring visual proof—they made a list of all the 'walking dead' and ordered the graves to be opened immediately. Each body was found in the same remarkable state of preservation as that of the old man, weeks before: by unanimous agreement the same grim ceremony was performed.

Dusk was falling as the last of the 'exorcised' coffins was replaced in its grave. In the sanctuary of the church, villagers, soldiers, and investigators waited tensely, watching from doors and windows—but nothing stirred. The 'army of corpses' had been routed for ever. . . .

In the years that followed the story became so garbled and confused that Cadreras frequently found himself the subject of derision, angry criticism and even, on occasions, accusations of witchcraft and necromancy. He appealed to the Royal Court to make some public statement which would save his reputation and make the facts clear—but the Emperor, on the advice of religious leaders and statesmen remained silent. It was feared that any such proclamation would cause a renewal of the panic which had swept the nation at the time of the occurences—and which had led to the desecration of hundreds of cemeteries in country districts.

So the Count de Cadreras became a social outcast. . . . and then an exile. Ten years after the sensational events he presented himself at Fribourg University to set down the plain, unadorned facts—determined to preserve his honour at least in the eyes of later generations.

Long after his death researchers, intrigued by the Fribourg document, tracked down the signed reports of the Royal Commissioners who had accompanied him on that last visit to Haidam —and found irrefutable confirmation. But it was in vain that they sought some explanation in keeping with the laws of Nature. . . .

Today we have reviewed the evidence—'sensible, circumstantial, and complete', to quote Montague Summers' assessment of it in *The Vampire in Europe*. Can this age of enlightenment provide a likely answer to the riddle? Or do we have to admit defeat and accept the supernatural explanation—that a legion of ghosts, with all the vitality and 'solidity' of the living, returned from the tomb to claim their kinsmen as companions in Death. . . . ?

Unsolved Mysteries, by Valentine Dyall.

Were the people of Haidam visited by relatives from beyond the grave or were they caught in the grip of something more natural but equally terrifying. Valentine Dyall gives his explanation of the mystery. . . .

ERGOT POISONING?

In August 1951, the French Government rushed medical teams and leading scientists to the little village of Pont Saint Esprit, on the River Rhône, to investigate the outbreak of a strange and dreadful malady: men, women, and children were reported 'suddenly taken with madness, suffering terrifying hallucinations, and attacking their relatives'.

The investigators found the village 'like a miniature bedlam'. Victims ran about the streets frothing at the mouth, screaming that 'ghosts and demons' were after them, and that they were being 'eaten alive by burning snakes'. Many attempted suicide, and the more serious cases had to be put in strait jackets.

Five people died in physical and mental agony, and more than thirty suffered 'temporary insanity' before the epidemic was checked. The scientists established the cause as 'poisoning, originating from an unidentified toxin contained in bread'. A local miller was arrested—and very nearly lynched!—on charges of buying, direct from farmers, quantities of 'black market' grain which had not undergone government inspection.

Though it was never officially announced, many of the scientists and physicians declared in 'off the record' interviews that the Pont Saint Esprit epidemic was an instance of ergot poisoning —a common scourge throughout Europe in medieval times, but increasingly rare since then.

The *Oxford Dictionary* defines ergot as 'a disease of rye, caused by fungus'. Medical text-books tell us that today the diseased seed is used in the manufacture of certain medicines.

This modern French report of 'a village gone mad' has much in common with the eighteenth-century Austrian records which describe 'the mystery of Haidam'. In both instances a small community was suddenly thrown into a state of terror, apparently healthy individuals suddenly fell ill and died, and many victims were convinced that 'ghosts' were pursuing them.

This leads us to ask why, if the 'hauntings' of Haidam were really only hallucinations resulting from ergot poisoning, the Count de Cadreras and the distinguished members of the Royal Commission failed to discover the truth? This apparent problem is readily solved by the realisation that in all probability they were themselves victims of the toxin and were suffering from a mild form of the disease throughout the inquiry! Unlike the twentieth-century investigators who rushed to Pont Saint Esprit in motor-cars, the Count de Cadreras and his colleagues would travel slowly, entering the affected zone gradually. While still some miles from Haidam—the 'epicentre'—they would be almost certain to consume infected grain in meals or refreshments obtained at inns or farmhouses.

The Austrian Commissioners knew nothing of hygiene, and little of enteric diseases. The modern French investigators, on the other hand, would automatically begin by taking precautions against food poisoning or impure water supplies, and probably made a point of eating all their meals at the hospital, several miles from Pont Saint Esprit, where the victims were taken for treatment.

Two problems remain—the remarkable preservation of the bodies in the Haidam churchyard and the fact that after the exorcism ceremony the 'hauntings' immediately stopped.

The former may be accounted for as the work of the toxin, part of the whole hallucination: the second is best explained as sheer coincidence—the outbreak simply happened to end in the hours following the exorcism, perhaps because the sudden influx of visitors (i.e. the Royal Commission and their retinue!) had helped clear up the last stocks of infected bread!

We must remember that suggestion plays an important part in mass hallucinations of this type. Once the idea of 'walking dead' was impressed upon the villagers, it was bound to influence the form of delusion experienced by future victims. The same peculiarity was observed at Pont Saint Esprit, where the visions and obsessions of the early victims formed a definite behaviour pattern for those that followed.

Unsolved Mysteries, by Valentine Dyall.

Was it ergot poisoning? Or were the people of Haidam visited by the ghosts of their long dead relatives?

You have now read the evidence. Do ghosts exist in their own right, or are they nothing more than waking dreams—just figments of our imaginations?

The Loch Ness Monster

Loch Ness never gives up its dead. (A Scottish saying)

Something rose from the water like a monster of prehistoric times, measuring a full thirty feet from tip to tail. It had a long sinuous neck and a flat reptilian head. Its skin was greyish black, tough looking, and just behind, where the neck joined the body, was a giant hump like that on a camel, though many times bigger.

Mr Alex Campbell, Loch Ness Water Bailiff.
Everybody's Magazine. Quoted by Tim Dinsdale in *Loch Ness Monster.*

An unusually fine view of the Loch Ness Monster was had by the captain, mate, and five of the crew of the steam tug *Arrow.* 'When passing up Loch Ness, two and a half miles east of Urquhart Castle,' said Captain Brodie of Leith in an interview, 'the mate and myself noticed a huge black-coloured animal rather like a hump-backed whale emerge on the loch surface and keep pace with the ship at some distance. We at once realised it was the Monster. We were honestly astounded at seeing such a huge creature in an inland loch, but, believe me, this was no whale, because just behind the foremost hump was another, and no whale on earth ever had two distinct humps.' By this time all the crew except a fireman had gone on deck to see the Monster, but only in time to watch it dive below.

YOU BE THE JUDGE

In a few moments it reappeared and in the captain's own words the second appearance was even more astonishing than the first, as the creature now showed seven humps or coils and tore past the tug at a terrific speed just on the surface. The coils, according to a deck-hand, reminded him of a giant serpent glistening brightly in the sunshine. The loch was almost calm, but the waves set up by the Monster were amazing, said Captain Brodie. As for the creature's length as it raced past the ship only a short distance away, the captain and his son testified that it was at least half as long as the tug, that is thirty to forty feet long. Captain Brodie said he was so impressed by what he saw that he made a special entry of the incident in the ship's log.

The Scotsman. August 31st 1938.
Quoted by J. A. Carruth in Loch Ness and Its Monster.

The case of the Monster in Loch Ness is worthy of our consideration if only because it presents a striking example of mass hallucination.

E. G. Boulenger. Observer. October 29th 1933.

The most famous case of the unsubmitted specimen is that of the 'Loch Ness Monster', in which the ingenuity of suggestions as to the nature of the animal concerned has been equalled only by the powers of imagination of some observers.

Scientific Research. British Natural History Museum.

I'm not saying whether I believe in the Monster or not—though I'm bound to admit that I'm more sceptical than when I first came up here. But there is that residue of evidence: the eye-witness reports; the strange wave patterns on the surface of the loch that can't be explained away. The Loch Ness Phenomena Investigation Bureau will go on examining that kind of evidence. . . . If you are there, Nessie, all we can do is congratulate you on evading our attempts to find you. As our sonar screens grow dim and our noise-makers fall silent, we leave you to a sound you may perhaps prefer, the music of the pipes.

Richard Lindley. Reporting from Loch Ness for Independent
Television News.

The existence of a herd of monsters in Loch Ness is a mystery which has puzzled man for the past fourteen hundred years and the problem is no nearer a solution today in spite of the advances that have been made in underwater detection techniques. There have been three thousand accepted sightings over the last thirty-six years.

106

THE LOCH NESS MONSTER

Situated in Inverness-shire, Loch Ness is the largest lake in the British Isles, measuring over 22 miles in length and averaging just under a mile in width. There is an estimated 263,000 million cubic feet of water in the loch reaching a maximum depth of 754 feet.

Many schemes have been suggested for 'netting' Nessie—the most drastic involved passing a strong electric current through the water in order to stun the Monster and bring it floating to the surface. The idea was squashed by the local fishery board. Another idea was to drain the loch completely!

The uniqueness of the Monster is acknowledged by an act of Parliament which guarantees it protection should it be caught. Bertram Mills's Circus made an offer of £20,000 for a live specimen and a New York zoo put up the sum of £5,000 for its capture. In spite of all attempts, Nessie has so far eluded the hunter.

A composite picture of the monster has been compiled by Tim Dinsdale, an aviation engineer, who studied 'one hundred separate eye-witness reports, obtained over twenty-six years, from various sources; commencing in May 1933.' Here are his findings.

IDENTI-KIT FOR A MONSTER

1. *Year of appearance*

The Monster appeared consistently during this period of time, and although the great majority of reports stem from the years 1933 and 1934, there is no real significance in this fact, and it is pointless to quote statistics. In the early thirties the Monster was not considered to be a joke, and people were not afraid to speak of what they had seen. Furthermore, due to the felling of trees and construction work, more of the loch was seen by more people than ever before, or since, and in consequence, more reports were recorded.

The important thing really is that reports have continued to come in right up to the present day, and the fact that these now only represent a small proportion of actual sightings (which is certainly the case) demonstrates to what extent the Monster has fallen into disrepute.

2. *Month seen*

Statistics for sightings: January—3. February—4. March—10. April—10. May—7. June—9. July—14. August—16. September—5. October—5. November—6. December—6. 'Summer'—3. 'Autumn'—2.

These figures are of course based on the hundred reports under consideration, and although it is plain that the Monster is seen all the year round, no firm conclusion can be drawn as to when it most commonly appears.

In winter, the loch is viewed almost exclusively by the local population, who rarely speak of the Monster even if they see it, whereas in summertime, there are visitors in hundreds, but, in summer, the leaves are on the trees, and along two-thirds of the roads surrounding the loch it is not possible to see the water, whereas in winter it is, in places. It is variables of this kind which invalidate the figures quoted above, but there *is* evidence to suggest the Monster has a preference for sunshine, or more properly perhaps, warm water, and in summer the water on the surface of the loch is several degrees warmer than that below, so—taking everything into consideration, it appears that summer months are probably best for viewing.

3. *Time of day*

Statistics: eighty-five per cent of surface appearances occur between dawn and 9.30 a.m.

This characteristic is quite clear cut, and important for two reasons. From a zoological point of view, it suggests the presence of a nocturnal animal, and from a practical viewpoint it provides a definite period of time each day, during which the odds against seeing it are reduced. It is, however, occasionally seen at all times throughout the day as well.

4. *The head and neck*

Statistics: Described in forty-three per cent of recorded sightings.

The following descriptive excerpts are but a few of many: 'A horse-like head with a long neck—serpent-like head, diameter not greater than neck—long undulating neck, slightly thicker than an elephant's trunk—head the size of a cow's, but flatter, visible neck about five feet long and one foot thick—head and face the size of a large dog, but definitely, snake-like—face like a goat, two stumps on top of head like sheep's horns broken off—eyes like slits in a darning needle—flat reptilian head, which it shook vigorously from side to side—head hardly wider than neck in profile, turned together from side to side—eyes large and glittering—like a huge swan with body submerged—Monster with huge long neck rose from the water'—etc.

The comparisons made with the heads of other animals inevitably differ to some extent, but if the matter of profile is given due consideration, they are not so much at variance after all. The majority of descriptions seem to refer to a definitely reptilian type of head though modified to include a snout and a most curious pair of 'horns' or protrusions occasionally seen on top of the head, exactly like those of a giraffe or a snail. The reported size of the head varies from one account to the next also, but it should be remembered that over water, both distance and scale are very hard to judge.

On occasions, white markings have been observed on the throat and cheeks. The mouth has been estimated at twelve to eighteen inches in width, and has been watched opening and closing every two seconds or so, as though the animal was breathing; and once, 'a kind of steam' was seen to issue from its mouth, and was blown back by the wind.

The most pronounced characteristic of the head is that it is *tiny* in relation to the enormous body to which it belongs and in profile it is hardly thicker than the neck itself; indeed, some witnesses fail to distinguish the head, as it seems no more than an extension of the neck, but those that do, at close quarters all seem to agree that it is very ugly and like that of a reptile—flat on top, and usually without evidence of eyes, but when the eyes *are* seen they are said to be like slits, near the top of the head, although they are occasionally referred to as being very large indeed, and glittering or luminescent; but whatever the most fitting description may be, one thing appears to be certain, they are not the eyes of a fish. The eyes of a fish are round, whereas those of a reptile are lenticular in appearance.

All things considered the head of the animal is of particular zoological interest and importance, and no less the neck, which exhibits equally puzzling characteristics. When the head and neck break surface they are usually carried at an angle of thirty degrees or so to the water, when the animal is moving at any speed, and only a foot or two may be showing, but on other occasions the neck protrudes at a very upright angle, the line of which is carried on by the head, rather in the fashion of an outraged farmyard gander, stretching its neck while hissing in defiance. In this position, which is by no means unusual, the neck is often described as a black pillar, or pole-like object streaking through the water, with spray breaking from it very much as it does from the bows of a ship. Estimates of height above water are almost invariably five to six feet and the thickness is generally thought to be about a foot, but it tapers towards the head and at the other extremity where it joins the massive body, it thickens very suddenly.

Occasionally the neck emerges slowly from the water, without any visible indication of the body behind it, and in this position the head and the neck present a graceful almost swan-like appearance, and people comment on its poise and balance. On several occasions, the head has been seen to turn rapidly from side to side 'as quick as a hen' or to shake itself vigorously, giving the appearance of acute awareness both of sight and sound; and there is evidence to suggest the latter sense may in fact be well developed. There must be at least a dozen recorded accounts which suggest the animal reacts immediately to sound—to a shouted exclamation, or the noise of a motor-boat engine, causing it to dive at once.

Taking into account the angle at which the neck is held, or the graceful arch when motionless in the water, and the consistent reference to a height of five to six feet above the water, total length of the neck must be nine or ten feet, and in view of its sinuous flexible movements it must be extremely muscular; a solid pillar of muscle springing from a tremendous breadth of shoulder, two to three feet thick at its base perhaps, then tapering down suddenly before continuing out to the head with an almost parallel thickness.

It is a very remarkable neck and if people are to be believed it is quite unlike that of any known *living species*—fish, mammal, or reptile, and there is no doubt that irrefutable proof of its existence will provide a very tough morsel for scientists to chew upon.

5. *The mane*

Statistics: Reference is made to a mane, or neck frill of some sort, in five per cent of sightings.

It seems just too much to expect that the fabulous 'water horse' should exhibit a mane—in addition to its other astonishing features, but if reports are studied impartially, there does appear to be some sort of appendage attached behind the head and neck which is quite distinct when seen, though it is not often reported; but perhaps this can be explained by the fact the animal is so rarely seen at close quarters.

On different occasions the mane has been described in the following words: 'like a small frill on top of the neck—saw something like hair or wool on the back of the neck.—Something extended four feet down the back of the neck from the head; dark coloured, rather like a mane.—The head and neck seemed to be covered with some sort of entangling substance.—At the back of the neck there was a curious fin.'

If we are to believe reports at all, we must not accept only those which fit the 'conventional' (if that is the word to use) pattern of sightings, and discard the others which do not. Each report must be carefully studied and with regard to the mane in particular this principle must stand, because upon it depends a link with later evidence of particular significance.

For the moment therefore it is well to remain content with a temporary acceptance of what appears to be highly improbable recalling to mind the fact that a 'frill' is displayed on the neck and back of some of the larger lizards. The Iguana for example, and the ancient Tuatara of New Zealand, both of which, of course, belong to the reptile family.

6. *The body*

Statistics: In twenty per cent of sightings, a back or body is reported as distinct from the appearance of humps, and the most common description is that of 'an upturned boat', but others have said: 'It looked like an elephant's back—stood about four feet high and ten to twelve feet in length—an egg-shaped body—seen end on there is a distinct angle at apex of back—a long dark body—like a gigantic eel twenty-five feet in length and five feet in diameter.'

Descriptions such as these are not very specific and the best that can be said for them is that the majority refer to some very large object.

7. *The humps*

Statistics: 'Humps' appear in no less than forty-five per cent of sightings, but these must be subdivided because the number of humps vary in quite an extraordinary manner. From amongst these forty-five separate statements, eight refer to one hump, nineteen to two, nine to three, and the remainder to a varied number of humps or 'coils' up to a counted total of twelve! At first sight it does not seem possible to explain this part of the riddle, and it is as well not to try—not until the subject has been studied in much greater detail, but it can do no harm to assess the size and shape of these remarkable protruberances.

Generally speaking, there appears to be three basic triangular humps, the largest in the middle, standing three to four feet above the surface, five to six feet in length at the water-line, and separated by six to eight feet of clear water from the other two humps. This adds up to an overall visible length of thirty feet or so. The humps, when seen, appear to be quite definitely structural and solid, like a 'steep-gabled house'. The angle subtended is almost a right angle, and when viewed in this position it seems that they cannot possibly relate directly to the backbone. They are not vertical undulations, and they are not fins. In all the hundred reports, no one has ever referred to a hump as a fin. Probably the only certain thing about them is that they are most peculiar, and a complete stumbling block to science. No known animal is capable of producing such a body shape—but the mystery does not end here.

The evidence states quite clearly that the humps vary in number, shape, and size, and that on occasions these changes have actually been watched taking place! Sometimes rounded humps are seen, instead of triangles and then again a whole collection of minor humps in a row; and the animal has been seen to swim off with three humps clearly in evidence and then return a few minutes later with no visible humps at all!

Unbelievable though it may seem, there can be little doubt that the visible parts of the *back* of the animal are capable of changing shape.

8. *Limbs, fins, or flippers*

Statistics: Mentioned in thirteen per cent of sightings.

In the majority of cases only the splashes are noted, but on three occasions the forward flippers have been actually seen out of the water, by different people.

This is a matter of considerable zoological importance, and if it is possible to establish beyond doubt that the animal has flippers or paddles instead of limbs it may help to lessen the doubt about its identity or the original species to which it is related. This is an important point, but recorded descriptions are not always clear.

'Saw front paddles working alternately as it turned about— saw what might have been limbs or flippers beating the water— saw two fore flippers extended but not being moved—considered there was evidence of paddling movement fore and aft and on either side—short legs or flippers—the wash was generated from a point behind the head and again from behind the second hump, as if powerful flippers were at work.'

Verbal reports like these are not sufficiently explicit and more concrete evidence must first be obtained before the matter is decided, but from what people have said it appears probable the Monster uses flippers or paddles to propel it through the water, and furthermore that the rear pair are larger than those at the front.

9. *The tail*

Statistics: Reported in eleven per cent of sightings.

Descriptions of a tail are relatively few in number, but are generally quite specific; for example:

'I saw the tail distinctly causing a great commotion, thrashing the water with much force—tail thrashed water like a propeller—

he thought that a powerful tail could be seen moving from side to side below the surface—commotion in water about fifteen to twenty feet behind last hump—two humps came into view and the whole length of tail could be seen on the surface, he judged the Monster to be eighteen to twenty feet long, the tail being about six feet long.'

The presence of a tail, once more is of great interest, and also the fact that it appears to be used in swimming. On one occasion only has it actually been seen out of the water, and on that occasion the estimate of length coincided with that recorded above—six feet, but in both instances the animal was thought to be no more than twenty feet in length overall, and as so many estimates of size suggest another very much bigger animal lives in the loch, it would be reasonable to expect its tail to be rather longer. In the second from last excerpt recorded above, a commotion was noticed fifteen to twenty feet behind the *last hump*; an estimate that compares with several other reports.

10. *Size or length*

In no less than thirty-three per cent of sightings specific reference is made to size, and, in the graphic words used in these reports it is possible to gain some impression of the enormous bulk of body.

'Estimated forty feet in length was showing—great size and bulk; length about thirty feet—huge creature about thirty feet in length—tremendous creature—tremendously long dark object—full thirty feet—it was a really huge creature—it was very great—must be of huge proportions—thirty to forty feet of it,' etc.

It is true to say that distance and scale are very difficult to judge correctly over water, but people have seen the animal, on occasions, at a distance of but a few yards, and there is no doubt at all that it is very, very large indeed—quite literally a Monster!

11. *Colour*

Specific reference twenty-eight per cent.

From amongst these reports two colours are reported consistently—elephant or battleship grey, and reddish brown; both these colours are referred to with equal frequency and in quite definite terms.

A few people have said the Monster is an olive green, a greenish black, black, or just dark in appearance, but in the latter case poor light, distance, or shadows may have obscured the true colour to some extent. There is some evidence to suggest that there may be a whitish strip down the throat, and in one instance white marks were seen on the 'cheeks' of the face at a distance of no more than forty yards. Beneath the water-line the colour of the body is sometimes said to be lighter than those parts showing above, but taking a cross-section of all these reports one can only conclude the animal is either able to change colour at will, or that colour varies with age or sex. The ability to change colour is characteristic of reptiles, but as no one has actually seen this happening, it seems more probable the two most usual colours, brown and grey have something to do with age or sex. A live crocodile, swimming in the water, could fittingly be described as greenish black, with lighter underparts, but to make comparisons of this sort may well be misleading, and the issue cannot be decided until a clear sequence of colour film is obtained at relatively close quarters.

12. *Skin or scales*

Specific reference fifteen per cent. *None* of these reports refer to scales, and of those that mention texture about one half say the skin appears smooth or glistening and the other half say it is rough, like that of a toad, or an elephant:

'Loathsome texture, reminiscent of a snail—rough looking —tough looking—skin dark and glistening—not smooth—like that of an elephant—not hairy—not glossy—skin glistening and fairly smooth—hide was something like that of an elephant or an immense toad,' etc.

The one thing about which all these reports agree is that it is *skin*, but bearing in mind the effects that light and shade, wetness and dryness could have on any surface viewed at a distance, it would be well to reserve judgement about texture, but at the same time there is one valid argument which suggests the skin may in fact be rough rather than smooth: a rough wet surface seen at a distance with the sun shining on it might appear shiny, and therefore smooth, whereas a smooth surface, wet or dry, would never appear rough.

Another point worth noting in these accounts is that no one has ever referred to fur, or bristles, or hair of the type one might expect to find on the back of a seal, and this is important because a theory had been put forward in the past suggesting the Monster may be a type of giant long-necked seal, which has somehow got into the loch.

It is perhaps too easy to draw a parallel between the 'toad-like' appearance of the skin and the many reptiles that possess this sort of covering, and although on the face of it it is conceivable it may turn out to be a reptile, one might be equally inclined to call it a mammal on the strength of similar comparisons made with an elephant's hide. Again, there is really not enough evidence on which to base conclusions, but the little that exists suggests a tough or warty hide on the body only. The neck is invariably reported as being smooth, and shining when wet.

13. *Human reaction*

The information contained under this heading is difficult to analyse unless one is prepared to include a 'factor' for astonishment, because in this column people's reactions have been noted carefully, and these are some of the comments made: 'Fantastic creature—the most extraordinary form of animal—appearance like a huge caterpillar (multi-hump position)—marvellous sight—remarkable creature—huge creature in a fury, lashed about—strange creature—a most amazing beast—like a monster of prehistoric times—petrified with astonishment—never seen anything like it before—an amazing sight—like a prehistoric monster in a school book—an astonishing sight quite unlike anything I have ever seen,' etc.

If these are false impressions—lies—there must be many liars, but from amongst the mass of more usual evidence human reaction can also be measured in terms different to those of mere astonishment. At a distance, people are sometimes awestruck by what they see—the very strangeness of the Monster, the graceful way in which it rides the waters of the loch; its size and amazing turn of speed all combine to present a picture so entirely different to anything before experienced, that those who witness it are much affected—but at really close quarters this sense of awe is sometimes turned to one of fear, and of the relatively few people who have seen the beast at really close quarters, some are not ashamed to admit to being very much afraid.

14. *Speed*

In thirty-seven per cent of reports people make some reference to speed, and the majority state the Monster is capable of almost unbelievable speed—but it is also fond of lolling or basking on the surface, and has been watched enjoying itself in this manner for periods of up to forty minutes.

'Cruising along at twenty to thirty miles per hour—motionless for ten minutes—swimming at a furious rate—loafing in the water—lay basking on the surface—terrific speed like a motor boat—slow moving, then suddenly dashed forward with incredible speed—kept pace with the Monster at twenty-five miles per hour in my car—had never seen anything travel on water so fast, it streaked across the loch—speed about thirty-five miles per hour—tremendous speed—faster than a fast motor boat—racing through water at terrific speed,' etc.

Reading these accounts in greater detail, two other characteristics come to light: the animal is inclined to suddenly 'dash' off, and when it does, it travels dead straight or in a gentle curve, but when it is paddling slowly, it often zigzags about as if undetermined where to go. Furthermore, if accounts of great speed are to be believed, it must possess enormous strength and a very good hydrodynamic shape, allowing its great bulk to slip through the water with minimum resistance.

15. *Wash or wake*

Statistics: forty-four per cent reference.

As might be expected almost every other report refers to the wash the animal creates.

'V-shaped wash in straight line at speed of outboard motor-boat—big splash—churning mass of white foam—parting water from its neck like a motor-boat—V-shaped wash; disturbance like that from a small ship—turmoil of water, miniature tidal wave—terrific commotion—leaving wake like that from a torpedo —sending up waves like a speed boat—waves like a steamer— big V wash, clearly visible at eighteen hundred yards—tremendous streak of white foam—an area four hundred yards in diameter in turmoil—wash like a powerful speed boat,' etc.

Disturbances like these would never be made by a small animal —on the contrary, they suggest the presence of something quite extraordinarily large and powerful.

16. *Dive or submergence*

Statistics: twenty-five per cent reference.

In reading reports about the Monster it is apparent there is something very odd about the way it disappears—something very odd indeed, so strange in fact it warrants the closest study, and if the remarks recorded under this heading appear repetitive, they are nonetheless worth noticing because they clearly prove a point which is of great significance—the Monster, though capable of diving in the manner that might be expected of it, head and neck first, followed by the body—only does so when suddenly frightened. Statistics show that in eighty-eight per cent of noted disappearances it *sinks vertically,* almost without a ripple.

'It turned sharply and sank—disappeared—then sank—it sank—then it sank—sank instantaneously—dived immediately when boats appeared—it sank down slowly as a whole, the relative position of head and neck remained unchanged—gradually sank—turned sharply, as though startled by the shouting and *plunged* beneath the water—sank perpendicularly—lowered its long neck and dived (on hearing approach of herring drifters) —it sank quite suddenly—submerged perpendicularly.'

In assessing these many similar statements, there can be no doubt that the Monster is able to sink straight down at will; and very rapidly too. This is quite extraordinary, and can only be explained in one of three ways. Either it forces its buoyant body underwater by displacing water upwards with its flippers, or, it alters its specific gravity—the density of its flesh and bones, or, it alters its actual displacement—by getting bigger or smaller.

The first possibility can certainly be ruled out, because it 'sinks without a ripple', and the second is very hard to conceive, but the third provides a ready answer, and fits nicely into place when the facts are considered—the facts of the variable number of humps, and the ability to visibly alter shape. If the humps are in fact inflatable air sacs capable of being pumped up or let down at will it would explain two parts of the riddle—the differing number of humps reported and the ability to sink. This is all very encouraging; and it is true that the ability to inflate auxiliary air sacs is a noted characteristic of both the fish and reptile family—but there is still one serious problem; people who see the triangular humps at close quarters invariably state they look solid and structural, a part of the beast itself, and definitely *not* like air sacs, and this ruins the theory completely.

Loch Ness Monster, by Tim Dinsdale.

The following is the first recorded story of a Monster in Loch Ness. Reminiscent of the monster stories of myth and legend, its main purpose is to demonstrate the remarkable powers of Saint Columba rather than give us an accurate picture of Nessie . . .

THE SAVAGE MONSTER

Of the driving away of a certain water monster by virtue of the prayer of the holy man. At another time again, when the blessed man (Saint Columba) was staying for some days in the province of the Picts, he found it necessary to cross the river Ness; and when he came to the bank thereof he sees some of the inhabitants burying a poor unfortunate man, whom, as those who were burying him themselves reported, some water monster had a little while before snatched at as he was swimming, and bitten with a most savage bite, and whose hapless corpse some men who came in a boat to give assistance, though too late, caught hold of by putting out hooks. The blessed man, however, on hearing this, directs that some one of his companions shall swim out and bring to him the boat that is on the other side, sailing it across.

On hearing this direction of the holy and famous man, Lugne Mocumin, obeying without delay, throws off all his clothes except his undergarments, and casts himself into the water. Now the monster, which was not so much satiated as made eager for prey, was lying hid at the bottom of the river; but perceiving that the water above was disturbed by him who was crossing, suddenly emerged, and swimming to the man as he was crossing in the middle of the stream, rushed up with a great roar and open mouth.

Then the blessed man looked on, while all who were there, the heathen as well as the brethren, were stricken with very great terror; and with his holy hand raised high, he formed the sign of the cross in the empty air, invoked the Name of God, and commanded the fierce monster, saying, 'Think not to go further nor touch thou that man. Quick! Go back!'

Then the beast, on hearing this voice of the saint, was terrified and fled backwards more rapidly than he came, as if dragged by cords, although it had come so near to Lugne as he swam, that there was not more than the length of a puntpole between the man and the beast. Then the brethren, seeing that the beast had gone away and that their comrade Lugne was returned to them safe and sound in the boat, glorified God in the blessed man, greatly marvelling. Moreover also the barbarous heathen who were there present, constrained by the greatness of the miracle, which they themselves had seen, glorified the God of the Christians.

Saint Adamnan's Life of Saint Columba.
Quoted in Loch Ness and Its Monster, by J. A. Carruth.

We all know examples of stories which have grown with the telling. Is this just one more example of how an ordinary event such as Saint Columba rescuing a drowning man has grown over the years into an extraordinary story of the Saint driving away a Monster in order to emphasize the miraculous side of Columba's nature?

The present Monsters appear much more docile than their medieval counterparts and are renowned for their shyness and timidity.

Although most of the sightings have taken place while the Monsters were in the water, there are a few cases in which one has appeared on dry land . . .

THE LOCH NESS MONSTER

OUT OF THE WATER

On Friday January 5th 1934 Mr Grant was returning home from Inverness on his motor bicycle. The time was about one in the morning and the night had been dark, but as he approached Abriachan the sky cleared and the whole landscape was bathed in bright moonlight. This part of the road has since been reconstructed, but a distance of three miles from Lochend places the scene fairly accurately.

All at once, he noticed a large dark object on the right-hand side of the road, partly in the shadow of bushes. As he drew nearer, a small head was turned towards him, then, as if it had taken fright, a large animal crossed the road in two great bounds. The direction taken was diagonal and away from the onlooker; the creature then passed rapidly through the undergrowth on the left of the road and disappeared into the loch.

'I had a splendid view of the object. In fact I almost struck it with my motor-cycle,' said Mr Grant, 'it had a long neck and large oval-shaped eyes on the top of a small head. The tail would be from five to six feet long and very powerful; the curious thing about it was that the end was rounded off; it did not come to a point. The total length of the animal would be fifteen to twenty feet. Knowing something of natural history I can say that I have never seen anything in my life like the animal I saw. It looked like a hybrid. I jumped off my cycle and followed the animal, which had entered the loch with great speed. There was a huge splash and from the disturbance of the surface it had evidently made away before I reached the shore.'

Mr Grant marked the spot and went home where he awakened his younger brother, told him what he had seen, and made sketches there and then. In June 1955, recalling memories of the occasion, he said that the animal's method of progress on the road reminded him of a kangaroo. Of the four limbs, the front ones were flipper-like, comparatively small and were not being used; he had not seen the rear limbs plainly enough to say what kind they were excepting that, judging by the animal's movement, they must have been powerful. As mentioned before, the beast crossed the road in two great bounds, using the hind limbs to spring from with a horizontal movement; on reaching the other side, the speed was much increased. Memory of the event is still vivid in Mr Grant's mind, though for many years he has preferred to say nothing about it on account of the treatment, amounting almost to persecution, to which he was subjected at the time.

He says that the creature's rear quarters had an appearance

even more massive than represented in his own sketch and that he did not at any time describe toes on the hind limbs.

After the incident great play was made in the press about impressions of toe marks beside the loch. It was further reported that a heap of animal bones had been found close to the place where the creature entered the water—suffice it to say that the bones probably, and the footmarks certainly, were 'planted'. As mentioned above, Mr Grant made a careful inspection at the time and marked the spot, then informed friends in Drumnadrochit and went home; shortly after daylight he returned himself but found no trace of anything unusual, except some flattening of the grass.

The Loch Ness monster as seen (and sketched later the same day) by Arthur Grant, a veterinary student, in January 1934.

This witness described, in the course of various statements, 'a head rather like a snake or eel, flat at the top, the large oval eye, longish neck, and somewhat longer tail. The body was much thicker towards the tail than was the front portion. In colour it was black or dark brown and had a skin rather like that of a whale. The head must have been about six feet from the ground as it crossed the road, the neck three and a half to four feet long and the tail five or six feet long. Height from the belly to the back would be about four and a half feet and the overall length eighteen to twenty feet.'

Mr Grant made statements to the police and before a professional society.

In 1947, together with his wife, he saw the Monster again. This time it was in the one-hump position and in the water.

Six months before the last related experience, the Monster had been seen crossing a road in broad daylight by Mr and Mrs Spicer, with whom my personal acquaintance is one of correspondence only. Commander Gould wrote:* 'I visited Mr and

* *The Loch Ness Monster and Others*, by Commander R. T. Gould.

Mrs Spicer and heard their story—and I became and remain convinced that it was entirely *bona fide*; that they had undergone a most unusual experience which had left a lasting and rather unpleasant impression.'

Before the occurrence Mr and Mrs Spicer had not even heard of the Monster, for at that period news of the creature was rare in any but local newspapers.

On July 22nd 1933 they were driving together along the road between Dores and Inverfarigaig at a speed of about twenty miles per hour. They had been on holiday further north and were returning to London. (Mr Spicer was a Director of Todhouse, Reynard and Co., Davies Street.)

Approaching a slight rise they saw at the top of it 'the most extraordinary form of an animal' crossing. On account of the slope, the lower few inches of the creature could not be observed. The first thing they noticed was an undulating neck a little thicker than an elephant's trunk; the undulations were rapid and showed two or three arches. The whole episode took place in a matter of seconds and the head was across the road almost before they saw it. The ponderous body crossed in a series of jerks, they saw no limbs and until afterwards did not realise that they must have seen the tail; at the time, the creature did not appear to have one. The tail was evidently curled round on the further side, its tip having the appearance of something being carried on the animal's back at the junction of the neck with the body. The creature stood about four feet high and the body was about the same length as the road is wide, that is ten to twelve feet (excluding the grass verge). It was about two hundred yards ahead of them when first seen; Mr Spicer put on speed, but by the time they reached the spot there was no sign of it. They heard no splash. The loch is here some twenty yards from the road and as the car accelerated any sound could have been drowned by the noise of the engine. They did not stop but saw an opening in the dense bushes where the creature had disappeared and made a point of speaking to the first person they met, a roadman, who told them about the Monster, adding that he was glad they had seen it, because people were laughing at a bus driver friend of his in Foyers who had reported seeing it from this same road. Mr Spicer said that he and his wife were both willing 'to take an oath or make any affidavit'—that it seemed futile to attempt to describe the creature because 'it was nothing like anything he had read about or seen. It was terrible, dark elephant-grey of a loathsome texture, reminiscent of a snail.'

The view of the loch at this part of the road is entirely obscured by a belt of bushes, hazel trees and alders forming a thick covering on the damp mossy bank to left and right.

Reports were circulated that the Monster had been seen 'with a lamb in its mouth'; this and other distorted or incomplete accounts were common at the time and, much to the annoyance of Mr and Mrs Spicer, were frequently repeated afterwards. As the creature crossed, it is not surprising that the tip of the tail looked something of an excrescence 'flopping up and down' at the front of the body, and it entered Mrs Spicer's mind for a moment that something was being carried on the creature's back. On reflection, Mr and Mrs Spicer decided that it must have been the end of the tail. It was only on second thoughts, too,

Impression of the Loch Ness Monster, as seen by Mr and Mrs Spicer of London, crossing the road near Dores, Inverness, in July 1933.

for the whole event was over in a matter of seconds, that they identified the thing like an elephant's trunk as a neck.

Mrs Spicer writes* confirming the above report and adds: 'I know there is a strange creature which went into the loch as we saw it, and I should be very pleased to hear that it has been identified. . . .'

More Than A Legend, by Constance Whyte.

Let us assume for the moment that there is no such creature as the Loch Ness Monster. Is there any other explanation for what Mr Grant, and Mr and Mrs Spicer saw crossing the road in front of them?

Various expeditions have set out for the loch determined to solve the mystery once and for all, either to capture the Monster in the flesh or on film, or to prove conclusively that it is an illusion, as insubstantial as the unicorn.

In April 1960, Tim Dinsdale undertook his own five-day survey of the Loch. Equipped with a battery of cameras and a telephoto lens that could film the Monster up to the range of a mile and over,

* Personal communication, May 1955.

he began a daytime search of the loch and its surroundings; spending his evenings interviewing local observers of the phenomenon.

A disturbance on the surface of the loch on the fourth day, convinced him that he was about to achieve the results he had hoped for. He decided to extend his stay in the area.

Then, on the sixth day, his patience was rewarded.

THE THRILLS OF THE CHASE

At dawn, on this last day of the hunt, I got up and repeated the usual pre-breakfast activities; watching first Borlum Bay from the heights above, and then from the northern shore opposite the horseshoe mark—waiting in hopes to see the Monster climb out of the loch in the manner the rumour had suggested —but without avail; and as the hours passed, I began to think of breakfast—the delicious sound and smell of frying eggs and bacon plagued my imagination, and my very empty stomach. At last I could stand it no longer and a few minutes before the accustomed hour set off back to Foyers, driving through the mountains along the single track I had come to know so well; past the little Loch Tarff, and the turning to Knockie lodge, then up and down and around about in a switchback of turns and gradients; finally climbing the hill behind the bay at Foyers, at the top of which the loch is seen once more.

A little before I approached this point I thought about the camera lying cushioned on the back seat. I knew that on the way down to the hotel I must pass within sight of the loch for a period of twenty or thirty seconds but although I knew the rules about maintaining a state of instant readiness when anywhere near the water, for a moment I was undecided. It seemed a lot of bother to mount the camera and tripod inside the car again for just these fleeting seconds, and I wanted breakfast badly—but, after a pause; when everything hung in balance, I decided to stick to the rigid drill which had become so much a matter of habit.

I stopped the car, and set up the tripod, next to the driver's seat, and putting the camera upon it, adjusted the friction clamps for movement in pitch and traverse. I took a light meter reading, and adjusted the lens aperture; checking also the focus, the turret setting, the viewfinder parallax, and frame, the cine camera speed and motor; and when all was in order trained the camera out of the window in a slightly downwards direction— repeating for the thousandth time the actions I had come to know as if by instinct.

I rolled slowly down the hill, with one hand on the tripod; glancing down towards the loch, stretched out in panoramic view two or three hundred feet below. The far shore, though just over a mile away, looked near enough to touch, and the black water between lay without a ripple upon it. The sun shone brightly, its rays unimpeded by the clear mountain air;—at a point approximately halfway down the road to the hotel, looking out at the water, I saw an object on the surface about two-thirds of the way across the loch. By now, after so many hours of intensive watching, I was completely familiar with the effect that distance had on the scale of the local fishing-boats, nearly all of which were built on common lines, fifteen feet or so in length, and the first thing that struck me immediately about the object was that although it appeared to be slightly shorter than a fishing-boat, at the same distance, it stood *too* high out of the water; and furthermore, with the sun shining on it brightly it had a curious *reddish-brown* hue about it which could be distinctly seen with the naked eye!

Unhurried, I stopped the car and raising my binoculars, focused them carefully upon it.

The object was perfectly clear and now quite large; and although when first I had seen it, it lay sideways on, during the few seconds I had taken with the binoculars it seemed to have turned away from me. It lay motionless on the water, a long oval shape, a distinct mahogany colour and on the left flank a huge dark blotch could be seen, like the dapple on a cow. For some reason it reminded me of the back of an African buffalo—it had fullness and girth and stood well above the water, and although I could see it from end to end there was no visible sign of a dorsal fin upon it; and then, abruptly, it began to move. I saw ripples break away from the further end and I knew at once I was looking at the extraordinary humped back of some huge living creature!

I dropped my binoculars, and turned to the camera, and with deliberate and icy control, started to film; pressing the button, firing long steady bursts of film like a machine gunner, stopping between to wind the clockwork motor. I could see the Monster through the optical camera sight (which diminished slightly) making it appear very clear indeed; and as it swam away across the loch it changed course, leaving a glassy zigzag wake; and then it slowly began to submerge. At a point two or three hundred yards from the opposite shore, fully submerged, it turned abruptly left and proceeded parallel to it, throwing up a long 'V' wash. It looked exactly like the tip of a submarine conning tower, just parting the surface, and as it proceeded westwards, I watched successive rhythmic bursts of foam break the surface—*paddle strokes*; with such a regular beat I instinctively began to count— one, two, three, four—pure white blobs of froth contrasting starkly against the black water surrounding, visible at eighteen hundred yards or so with the naked eye; denoting a tremendous power!

Awestruck, I filmed the beast as it proceeded westwards in a line as straight as an arrow, panning the camera to keep pace with it. I knew that having already exposed a length of film the day before there would not be much in reserve, and a quick look at the footage indicator proved this to be the case—I had only fifteen feet remaining. Faced with an appalling decision, and only seconds in which to make it, I stopped filming. The Monster was now a long way off, and going at considerable speed in a westerly direction. I glanced at the second hand of my watch again—in four minutes, the animal had swam nearly three-quarters of a mile, and was almost out of range; a mile-and-a-half away at least. I dare not risk these last few precious feet of film, because at any moment I knew it might come to the surface again, or as was so often reported, change direction, and come dashing back across the loch with head and neck upraised, and it was the head and neck I wanted. I had now recorded the wake on twenty to thirty feet of film and could add nothing useful to it, so I decided on a sudden gamble—I knew it would be possible to drive the car across a field, right to the water's edge at a point to the west of lower Foyers and that in so doing in just a very few minutes, two or three at most, I could get nearly a thousand yards closer to the Monster!

It was certainly worth the risk, and in seconds I folded up the tripod, and shot off down the steep zigzag road, going like a rocket —sounding the horn as I went, leaving a trail of dust. Over the bridge at the bottom, wheeling right I missed the entrance to the field, and cursing wildly carried on into a loop road round a group of houses, knowing it would prove the quickest way in which to double back.

I went round the tarmac circuit with tyres squealing, almost on two wheels, driving as I had never driven before in my life— and at the side of the road in front I saw a man look up: his face a mask of astonishment! Rounding the last bend and then down the track, I changed into lower gear and tore off across the grass, arriving at the shore in a matter of seconds later.

I jumped out eager to learn my fate; but one brief glance was enough to tell me I had lost both the race, and my exhilarating gamble—the loch was once again as tranquil as a pond! Climbing thirty feet or so up a bank I looked to left and right, searching the surface with binoculars for miles in each direction but there was nothing to be seen upon it; no sight or even sound of a fishing-boat, or other surface craft.

In the few minutes it had taken to race to the water's edge, the Monster had dived once more back into the depths, but before the dark waters closed over it again, it had given up to me a part—a little part—of its quite uncanny secret; and although I now knew the hunt was really over, I also knew without any lingering shadow of doubt I had at last succeeded—through the magic lens of my camera I had reached out across a thousand yards, and more, *to grasp the Monster by the tail.*

Loch Ness Monster, by Tim Dinsdale.

Kodak developed the film and the first showing was a thrilling experience for Mr Dinsdale. Although blurred by the distance, he could pick out 'the Monster's strange humped back' speeding away from the camera. After a few manoeuvres he watched it submerge and disappear from view heading in a parallel direction with the distant shore.

The film was eventually handed over to the Joint Air Reconnaissance Intelligence Centre, the experts employed by the R.A.F. to interpret their aerial photographs. They enlarged the film twenty times and reached the following conclusion. . . .

'The assumption is that it is not a surface vessel. One can presumably rule out the idea that it is any sort of submarine vessel, which leaves the conclusion that it is probably an animate object.'

They computed that whatever the nature of the 'animate object' on Mr Dinsdale's film, it was sixteen feet long and travelled at ten miles an hour.

The question that must be asked at this stage is just what *do* people see and film around Loch Ness. Hoaxes can be ruled out for to deceive such a large number of people a hoaxer would require a submarine, its superstructure shaped in the form of a monster, to be able to carry out his deception. Even supposing that these difficulties could be overcome, the hoaxer would have to berth and launch such a craft in complete secrecy and also ensure that it was in position on the loch in time to delude a gullible witness. Lies too cannot account for such a large number of sightings. It is a well-known fact that stories grow with the telling, each person adding to the original tale until it becomes unrecognisable but, as we saw from Mr Dinsdale's painstaking research, all the witnesses appear to be describing the same creature. Also many professional people have risked their reputations reporting what they have seen, knowing full well that they ran the risk of being ridiculed by the sceptics. And, as for achieving notoriety or financial gain from perpetrating such a lie, a large number of witnesses have preferred to remain anonymous, while others have had to spend a considerable amount of their own money buying the expensive photographic equipment needed.

Perhaps many of the sightings are due to natural phenomena such as the sunken waterlogged trunk of a tree which comes to the surface buoyed up for a while by gases produced in the decaying process. Once out of the water, the gas escapes and the log sinks once more into the loch. Or it could be the arrow-like wake of a boat, the two sides of the V spreading outwards until they reach the rocky shores of the loch, returning to the centre on the rebound and forming a furrow of water as much as half an hour after the boat has passed. Such a furrow of water when seen from a distance can appear to resemble the back of some aquatic creature. Or the 'Monster' could be a shadow on the film, or a shadow on the loch cast by the overhanging hills, or a mirage.

But there are some sightings which cannot be explained away as natural phenomena. And many experts are prepared to state categorically that what people are seeing is either a conventional creature such as a salamander, or a creature as yet unrecognised in zoological circles. The possibility of Nessie being a giant eel is ruled out by virtue of the fact that an eel travels through the water in a series of lateral undulations whereas the Monster takes a straight course; similarly, seals' movements and habits are vastly dissimilar from those exhibited by Nessie.

The most obvious explanation is that Nessie belongs to a completely unrecognised species of creature such as the sea serpent, fifty sightings of which have been reported since the end of the Second World War; or a large species of newt possessing a long neck.

But a much more convincing argument can be made out for the Loch Ness Monster being a type of prehistoric plesiosaur that has adapted itself within a breeding herd to the cold water conditions of the loch since it was cut off from the sea five to seven thousand years ago. The plesiosaur, a sea reptile, became extinct seventy million years ago. Measuring from ten to forty feet in length, it had a small lizard-like head on a long flexible neck. Its body was equipped with two pairs of long powerful flippers and the tail was thick and about the same length as the body. The possibility of such a creature surviving to the present day is not as incredible as it may seem for the coelacanth too was considered an extinct fish until one was caught in the Indian Ocean in 1938.

The Loch Ness Phenomena Investigation Bureau Limited on the other hand believe that Nessie must be some form of giant marine slug. This would account for the lack of skeletal remains, although the Loch has no tides to wash a corpse ashore and the vast layer of mud on the bottom of the Loch presumably disposes of much vital evidence.

One difficulty in finding the Monster in the loch has always been the extreme murkiness of the water, cloudy with peat brought down by the highland streams. Divers can see no more than ten feet ahead.

In 1969, determined to surmount even this barrier, Independent Television News spent nine months organising a vast complicated

On April 23rd, 1960, Tim Dinsdale filmed an object in Loch Ness from a range of about one mile. The film has been examined and reported on by experts. Four frames are given here. The two on this page show the object partially out of the water and submerged. The experts conclude that the object in the top picture is not a surface or a submarine vessel and is at least 6 feet in width and 5 feet in height.

The top picture again shows the object submerged. The bottom picture is from a film, taken for comparison purposes an hour later, showing a 14 ft boat with a 5 ft beam and a 5 horse power motor at full throttle. Note the different wake and the distinct propeller wash. By comparison with that of the boat, the wash in the top picture must be at least 1 ft 6 in high.

search of the loch involving sonar equipment, a time-phased camera hanging below a captive balloon, a midget submarine and batteries of film and television cameras with long focus lenses.

THE GREAT MONSTER HUNT

Thursday September 11th 1969
Loch Ness

Independent Television News next Sunday begins a fourteen day concentrated search for the Loch Ness Monster—the most sophisticated and scientific expedition ever mounted in the loch.

A team of scientific experts are now assembled at Loch Ness. They will be operating the special equipment for tracking down the Monster, or Monsters, and bringing them to the surface.

More than three thousand people have reported seeing the Monster. But no one has ever actually found the Monster or photographed it to show exactly what it looked like 'beyond all reasonable doubt'.

The ITN expedition, with over fifty men and women operating the latest underwater devices and keeping a dog-watch on cameras placed strategically round the loch, has the best chance to date of finding the answer.

Indications that there could well be a Monster were discovered last summer when a team from Birmingham University carried out a sonar search of the loch. Professor D. Gordon Tucker, who led the search then and heads the Birmingham University team in the ITN expedition, said at the time that a sonar reading in the depths of the loch made a further and more sophisticated investigation necessary.

Plessey are providing the sonar equipment to sweep the search area of the loch. The plan is to stretch a sonar 'curtain' vertical beneath the waters of the loch with a second sonar developing a horizontal scan.

Then the Monster or Monsters will be tempted into the sonar net by dropping a tasty dish of anchovy, blood meal, and gelatine, around the sides of the 'curtain'. Underwater noise-makers (evidence is that the Monster dislikes noise) mounted on launches will be converged on the sonar area, driving the elusive creature before them.

Both sonar points will be linked by radio and equipped with large-scale grid plots so that any sighting can be instantly fixed and tracked. Each sonar screen will be equipped with a 'slave' monitor which will be continuously filmed. All activities will be automatically tape recorded. The expedition is being carried out in conjunction with the Loch Ness Phenomena Investigation Bureau.

Members of the Loch Ness Phenomena Investigation Bureau will be scanning the loch for signs of the Monster. The sonar equipment will be able to pin point areas on which the ITN water-borne camera teams can converge.

Director of the L.N.P.I.B. is Mr David James, a former Conservative M.P. and a keen amateur naturalist. He founded the bureau after talks with naturalist Peter Scott who felt the Loch Ness Monster should be given serious consideration in the House of Commons. Mr James says: 'I only believe what I see and I haven't seen anything yet. But I am sure there is something there. I am absolutely hooked.'

Many people hold the theory that the Monster only surfaces for any length of time at night. So a sixteen millimetre camera is being adapted to take a new gun sight only just declassified that can 'see in the dark'. 'It gives an incredibly clear picture in the dark,' said an ITN spokesman.

Known as the Passive Night Sight, it has been developed for the British Army by Rank Precision Industries. Given reasonable conditions it can 'see' for a distance of five hundred yards. An ITN cameraman keeping watch through his camera linked to the sight, will simply film anything that looks unusual at night.

ITN reporter Richard Lindley has made five trips to Loch Ness this year to report on the earlier ground work carried out by the expedition.

It was during one of these trips that Lindley explored the underneath of the loch in a Vickers experimental submarine. One new fact that emerged from this underwater research was the loch was nearer a thousand feet deep, two hundred feet deeper than shown on the official map.

ITN's scientific interest has produced some new and interesting film from the public. Earlier this week News At Ten, the ITN half-hour nightly programme, showed some film taken by Mr Harvey Barsky, an American civil servant, which he shot last May. It shows something unusual moving in the water. Other film sent to ITN is now being studied by the Royal Air Force photographic intelligence unit.

The area round Temple Pier, from where the expedition conducts its operations, has taken on a festival air. Caravans for the expedition members are thronged round what is normally a quiet backwater of the loch. The main boat for the expedition, the *Jessie Ellen*, is gay with bunting. Everyone is in good spirits.

YOU BE THE JUDGE

Richard Lindley says it seems strange that while men can get to the moon and back we have still not established whether or not there is some unusual creature in the loch. 'This expedition has been planned with the hope of establishing once and for all if a Monster does exist,' he said.

The next fortnight will tell. If ITN do find the Monster the signature tune of the Apollo 10 and 11 astronauts may have to be rewritten. Instead of 'Fly me to the Moon' Frank Sinatra could be singing 'Fly me to the Loch'.

Independent Television News

But in spite of all the effort involved . . .

NESSIE BAFFLES THE BOFFINS

Loch Ness, September 27th—The ITN search for Nessie is drawing to a damp—and probably inconclusive—close. The Indian summer that smiled on the start of the expedition is over. Winds of over eighty miles per hour are sweeping the surrounding hills and lashing the loch waters into galloping ranks of white horses.

Winter is coming to Loch Ness—and it is a winter of discontent for those of us who thought we could tickle the Monster to the surface with our technological aids.

The twenty-four miles of the loch (average width one mile; depth in places over nine hundred feet; water volume two hundred and sixty-three thousand million cubic feet) have been scoured as never before.

The two sonar teams—the Plessey unit water-borne in the *Jessie Ellen* and the Birmingham University team based on the shore—have kept their day and night vigil in vain.

Not once did their display screens show even the briefest orange 'blip' which would indicate something unusual stirring in the loch.

In case some bleary-eyed sonar operator missed the vital moment, every movement on those screens has been filmed automatically with time-lapse cameras. A total of one hundred and forty-six thousand pictures was taken. Each one was examined by the sonar crews. Not one revealed anything strange.

The search pattern was varied. It began with the Plessey unit stationary in mid-loch—its *horizontal* beam criss-crossing with Birmingham's beamed *vertically* across the loch.

When that produced nothing Plessey's Mike Fidell, the technical operations manager, changed the tactics. The *Jessie Ellen* steamed up and down the loch, while the sonar transducer

This photograph gives the explanation of many reported sightings of the Loch Ness Monster. Monster-like humps can be formed by a boat's wake bouncing off the sides of the loch and meeting again in the middle, up to half an hour after the boat has passed.

was lowered at fifteen-minute intervals. But still no sign of Nessie.

Perhaps our noise-makers were driving her down to the bottom? Perhaps night sweeps would be more successful?

We changed our search pattern yet again. The noise-makers were withdrawn and on one calm, pitch-black night we spent six hours drifting as silently as we could through the darkness.

Cameraman Ken Taylor stood by with the night-sight. Through the view-finder of his sixteen millimeter Arriflex camera attached to this electronic device he could see five hundred yards of loch, bathed as if in sunshine.

Had anything surfaced within that range, he could not have missed it. But nothing surfaced. If Nessie is a nocturnal creature —this was her night off.

We sailed back to Temple Pier at dawn, baffled but not yet beaten. Perhaps the underwater TV camera would produce results?

Next day—off Urquhart Castle, where the Monster is reputed to lurk in underwater caverns—we lowered the camera into the peat-stained depths, and gathered expectantly round the monitor screens aboard the *Jessie Ellen*.

We had filmed the same area earlier this year—when Richard Lindley and cameraman Cyril Page went down in the Vickers' submersible *Pisces*. Then we got fascinating colour pictures of the barren loch-bed—an area never explored before.

This time, with the underwater TV camera swinging free, focused automatically from the *Jessie Ellen*, we hoped for even better things. But there was still no sign of Nessie. The only living thing we saw was one large eel—floating lazily across the screen.

If Nessie lives on eels—and wanted a change of diet—there was always our bait, laid in large quantities by Dr David Taylor, of the Flamingo Park Zoo at Malton in Yorkshire.

This, too, had no effect—although the four-man crew of a drifter, passing through the baited area, claimed to have seen something strange on the surface.

'We thought it was five large logs or tree trunks', they told us in Inverness that night. 'They were in two groups—one of three, one of two, and not wanting to ram them, we cut our engines. Then, as we were about a hundred yards away they disappeared, in a swirl of foam.'

An intriguing story. But without our own visual evidence we could hardly take it as proof of a Monster sighting.

Others tried to be helpful, too. Even if our efforts to find Nessie were unrewarding, the size of our postbag was proof of the interest in our nightly reports on News At Ten.

One sixth-former sent us his own thesis, convincingly written, superbly illustrated, suggesting that all photographs of the Monster are the product of a mirage, caused by the geological formation of the loch.

Class 2/5 at Slade Secondary Modern School, Bexhill, Kent fortified us with advice, drawings of Nessie as they saw her—and the comforting thought that we should not be 'too disappointed' if we didn't find the Monster.

Of course we *are* disappointed, some more than others.

Mike Fidell thinks that the sonar search was 'ninety-nine per cent effective' and tends to doubt the existence of any Monster. 'I don't see how it could have escaped our sonar beams.'

Cameramen Ken Taylor and John Corbett—even after spending hours peering fruitlessly through their view-finders—are less dogmatic. 'What about all those convincing eye-witnesses,' they say. 'You can't ignore them.'

Our sound recordists join the ranks of the doubters. 'A profitable fairy tale,' according to Ron Hubbard. And fisherman Eric Vincent adds: 'I don't know about the Monster—but the trout fishing is great.'

Project organiser Don Horobin, ITN Assistant Editor, has no doubts at all. 'For me—it's the end of a legend.'

Reporter Richard Lindley is not saying. He preserves the impartiality required of all ITN reporters.

As for me—I am still willing to believe the available evidence that points to the Monster's existence.

Nessie—in my view—remains more than a myth. Some passing tourist with a box brownie could yet surprise us all.

Eric Stevens. Loch Ness Programme Editor,
Independent Television News.

Can so many people be mistaken? Are the stories of a Monster deliberately invented to attract tourists to the area? Are all the sightings to be put down to waterlogged tree trunks, freak waves, the wake of boats, shadows on the water or on film? Is Nessie just a myth, a pleasant legend with no more substance than Saint George's dragon?

Or, are there Monsters in the loch? And did the sonar pings drive them to seek refuge in some deep underwater cavern?

If the Monsters do exist, to what species do they belong? Is it a salamander? A sea serpent? A type of prehistoric plesiosaur? Some form of giant marine slug? Or something else?

FLYING SAUCERS

One night at Walschied, a report suddenly spread that Martians had landed in a villager's garden. While the women fled into the church, dozens of Frenchmen seized guns and clubs and bravely closed in on the garden. There in the dark they could see the 'invaders'—small figures with glowing heads. The Frenchmen started to charge, when suddenly they realised the truth. The 'Martians' were huge chrysanthemums, each covered with white cloth for protection in case of an early frost.

The Flying Saucer Conspiracy, by Donald Keyhoe.

I believe they exist . . . more than ten thousand sightings have been reported, the majority of which cannot be accounted for by any 'scientific' explanation. No earthly materials that we know can be passed through the air at such a speed (nine thousand miles per hour) without getting too hot to allow human occupants to exist. The accelerations which they develop in starting, changing course, and stopping, would also make human life, as we know it, impossible. I say then that I am convinced that these objects do exist and that they are not manufactured by any nation on earth. I can, therefore, see no alternative to accepting the theory that they come from some extra-terrestrial source.

Air Chief Marshal Lord Dowding in the *Sunday Dispatch*.

FLYING SAUCERS

We found no direct evidence whatever of a convincing nature now existing for the claim that any UFOs represent spacecraft visiting Earth from another civilisation.

Dr Edward U. Condon. Scientific Study of Unidentified Flying Objects.

The Condon Committee has provided some valuable insights but its contributions to a solution of the UFO puzzle seem outweighed by its omissions. Before the committee ever was formed it was known that ninety-five per cent of all sightings could be explained either as hoaxes or as known natural or man-made phenomena. But while the report states: 'It is such a residual (the twenty-five per cent of unexplained sightings) that is the core of the UFO problem . . .' they did not solve this problem—the problem remains:

What are the UFOs?

The Condon Report Pro and Con, article in *Fate*, by John Ross.

THE EAGLE HAS LANDED

The lunar module was now approaching what should have been 'low gate', a point some five hundred feet above and two thousand feet east of the landing site. Pitched to nearly the vertical position, the lunar module was now 'standing' on its descent engine, dropping gently towards the landing area. Through his triangular window Armstrong could now see where aggs* was taking him: straight into a crater full of large boulders and 'big enough to house the Houston Astrodome'. Evidently they had arrived at 'low gate' some two miles short of the intended position. This may have been due to 'mascons', concentrations of mass hidden below the lunar surface. They are thought to be huge meteorites, of density greater than the rest of the lunar rock, which have been buried after impact, and give rise to a sudden increase in gravity that can draw spacecraft in low orbits perilously off course. Until the gravity maps of the moon are more perfect, even computers cannot guard against this peril.

Armstrong flicked a switch to give him full manual control and, summoning up all his flying experience, guided the ungainly monster to safety. With his right hand he controlled the sixteen attitude control thrusters while his left hand adjusted the thrust of the descent engine. Armstrong remained ice cool, his heart

* AGS ('aggs'): abort guidance system. Abort: The cutting short of a mission before it has accomplished its object.

rate a steady determined pace, as he edged the lunar module into
the last few seconds towards touchdown, checking its progress on
the attitude indicator, the altimeter, the various speed gauges,
and with quick glances out of the window.

Aldrin: '35 degrees (pitch) . . . 35 degrees . . . 750 (altitude) . . .
coming down at 23 (feet per second) . . . 700 feet, 21 down (feet
per second) . . . 33 degrees . . . 600 feet, down at 19 (feet per
second) . . . 540 feet, down at 30 (feet per second) . . . down at
15 . . . 400 feet, down at 9 . . . 8 (degrees, pitched) forward . . .
350 (feet), down at 4 . . . 330 (feet), $3\frac{1}{2}$ down . . . we're pegged on
horizontal velocity . . . 300 (feet), down $3\frac{1}{2}$ . . . 47 (degrees)
forward . . . $1\frac{1}{2}$ down . . . got the shadow (of the lunar module)
out there . . . down at $2\frac{1}{2}$ . . . 19 (pitch) forward . . . altitude
velocity lights . . . $3\frac{1}{2}$ down, 220 feet . . . 13 (pitch) forward . . .
11 forward, coming down nicely . . . 200 feet, $4\frac{1}{2}$ down . . . $5\frac{1}{2}$
down . . . 160 (feet), $6\frac{1}{2}$ down . . . $5\frac{1}{2}$ down, 9 (pitch) forward . . .
5 per cent (descent engine thrust) . . . 75 feet, things looking good
. . . down a half, 6 (pitch) forward . . .'

Mission Control: '60 seconds.' Aldrin: 'Down $2\frac{1}{2}$ . . . forward
. . . forward . . . good . . . 40 feet, down $2\frac{1}{2}$ . . . picking up some
dust . . . 30 feet, $2\frac{1}{2}$ down . . . faint shadow . . . 4 (pitch) forward
. . . 4 (pitch) forward, drifting to the right a little . . . 6 (forward
pitch), down a half.'

Mission Control: '30 seconds.' Aldrin: 'Drifting right . . .
contact light (landing probes attached to three of the pads of
the descent stage had touched the lunar surface, Armstrong
counted one second and punched a button to cut the engine) . . .
O.K., engine stop . . .'

Mission Control: 'We copy you down, Eagle.' Armstrong:
'Houston, Tranquility base here, the Eagle has landed.'

Peter Ryan: The Invasion of the Moon 1969.

And so, on July 20th 1969 Neil Armstrong and Edwin Aldrin
became the first men to land on an alien world. It was: 'One
small step for man, one giant leap for mankind.'

But is our own planet Earth being visited by aliens from other
worlds? Many people believe that it is. One of the greatest unsolved
mysteries of our time concerns the strange array of lights, flaming
crosses, cigar shaped craft, and flying discs reportedly seen by
observers throughout the world and referred to as unidentified
flying objects, UFOs for short. Take, for example, the following
graphic account by The Rev. Father R. Dean Johnson . . .

THE PRIEST AND THE SAUCER

We had no indication as we left home that Sunday evening that within a few minutes we would have one of the strangest experiences of a lifetime. May 19th 1963 was a beautiful spring evening. The sky was clear and the absence of a breeze made it less chilly than usual for that time of year near Lake Michigan.

Earlier in the evening we had visited a friend in the hospital. We drove along absorbed in our discussion of our friend's misfortune and how we might arrange our personal affairs so we could be of some help.

We had left home in Zion, Ill., and were on the western edge of Waukegan travelling south on Green Bay Road (Highway 131) about five miles south of the Illinois–Wisconsin line. This road runs parallel to Lake Michigan, following a ridge some four miles inland, so that driving this route, one gets a panoramic view of the lakeshore area near Waukegan.

It was about a quarter past ten at night when I happened to notice a bright white light off to the southeast, and called my wife's attention to it. She thought, except for its height and distance, it looked rather like a floodlight, such as is used at a ball park. It appeared to be stationary, and judging by the industrial smoke-stacks near the lake front, it must have been some six or seven miles out over Lake Michigan, and at an elevation of a couple of thousand feet or more. As the light appeared to get smaller, it became obvious that it was moving directly away from us, merely giving the illusion of being stationary.

In a few moments, however, it changed course, moving south-west as we continued driving south. As it came closer, it once again looked like a huge, somewhat elongated floodlight. I had been momentarily distracted by the oncoming traffic, when my wife excitedly said, 'It's on fire!' For just a moment, it looked as if it might be an aircraft about to crash.

By the time I could look up again, it obviously was not on fire, but was pulsating or flashing light, going off and on in a steady pattern. This was the only time when either of us felt even momentary fear. Our whole reaction was one of curiosity and excitement.

We were beginning to realise we were seeing a sight few have ever witnessed. We had heard reports of sightings of strange things before, but we never had given enough real thought to the phenomenon to decide whether or not we even believed such reports to be true.

By this time, the object was over northern Waukegan and

coming in lower. By the time we had driven another five miles it was close enough to see that it was not a single light, but several horizontally arranged lights—all of them white. As it continued to approach, we were startled to discover that they were not external lights, but windows, showing the interior of the craft brightly illuminated! Then the separate windows became more distinct. They were square! The entire object looked oblong, with windows on two levels, like the fuselage of a double-decker airliner, with the nose and tail chopped off square. There were no wings and no red or green lights, as is required of all authorised aircraft.

As it came to within a couple of miles of us, it seemed to be getting longer and shorter in a steady rhythm, like an accordion. It continued to glide smoothly towards the south-west.

As we crossed Highway 132, it was coming in towards us at very low altitude, and it was not until then that the various illusions became understandable. I drove another half mile, pulled off the road, and we both jumped out of the car as the strange craft passed slowly over our heads, close enough for us to see into the windows! There was just enough light from the highway and buildings to enable us to see its outline quite clearly. It was drum shaped, with vertical sides, so that seen in profile, it looked oblong.

I estimated it to be about two or three hundred feet above us, possibly eighty feet in diameter, and fifteen or sixteen feet high. The entire craft revolved counter-clockwise at approximately one-half revolution per second, and was gliding at the almost casual rate of about forty miles per hour, well above the tree tops.

The windows were evenly spaced all the way around on two levels, which appeared to be three feet across or slightly less, and horizontally spaced about that same distance apart. However, on each level there was a section which either had no windows, or else there was a compartment which was not illuminated. In one position, the upper left windows were dark, and the lower right were dark. As the craft revolved one hundred and eighty degrees, there were illuminated windows the full width on both levels. Hence, from a great distance, as the craft revolved it was alternately illuminated its full width and then only partially, which gave the accordion effect.

Unfortunately, although we were close enough to actually see into the windows, we could see nothing but ceiling, as we were looking up at an angle of perhaps sixty degrees. Even so, it was enough to get a definite sense of depth within the structural form.

Unless the craft was much higher than it appeared and therefore much larger in overall dimension, the ceiling height in each storey must have been no greater than six feet, depending upon the thickness of the floors and ceiling.

Because it was late evening it was difficult to get a clear idea of the shape of the underside or of the structural material. The lasting impression was its boxiness and angular lines. (I always had had a mental image of a 'flying saucer' as very sleek and streamlined, tapering out to a fine edge.)

There was something very eerie, about this strange craft, beyond its unusual appearance, that neither of us quite identified until later. This enormous vehicle, as large as our church, floating just over our heads, *was absolutely silent*! There was no sign of either mechanical or jet propulsion and there was no air disturbance such as would have been caused by any device similar in principle to a helicopter.

We got back into our car after it had passed by, and continued southward. Only a few hundred feet ahead, there was a stalled car on the shoulder of the road, and three men were bent over the fenders working on the engine. This huge craft had passed within a hundred yards of them without their noticing it!

Several other riders on the highway appeared to be following the course of the strange craft. A carload of boys went racing past us as one beat on the side of the car and yelled, 'Look at the flying saucer!' They too pulled their car off the road, as had others along the highway, in order to get a better look.

The lighted craft continued in a south-westerly direction perhaps another mile, then turned south-east again, gaining somewhat in altitude and velocity. It passed over Green Bay Road again and over North Chicago and on out over the lake again. Finally, turning south west, it continued this zig-zag pattern, still gaining in altitude. By the time we had driven another five miles or so, it appeared to be over Lake Forest or Highland Park, and we had to abandon the chase. In all, we had watched the craft for fifteen to twenty minutes.

Later that same evening, we talked with someone who had attended the stock car races at the Waukegan Speedway that evening, only about half a mile south of our closest sighting. Because of the bright floodlights there, the craft could not be seen as clearly, but it was seen. Comparing the angle and direction of his view, it seemed that my estimate of the elevation of the craft, at least, was relatively accurate.

I also tried calling the local newspaper and radio station that night, but there was no answer. I called again early the next morning and contacted Radio Station WKRS, Waukegan, to learn that there had been numerous reports of other sightings, but none so far had been at such close range. After an extended conversation, I was asked if I would consent to having my description tape recorded. I agreed and he said he would have to call me back from a phone with the recorder attached. In spite of the rather detailed report that I then gave, not one word was published by either the radio station or its affiliate, the *Waukegan News-Sun*! This was my first personal experience with what I later learned to be the Pentagon's effort to censor all such reports. Others who had seen the strange craft the same night we did, but from a greater distance, said they had called the police and other civil agencies and got a variety of improbable explanations.

At the time, I was priest-in-charge of All Souls Episcopal Church in Waukegan, and for several years we had published a weekly church newspaper. That week, I printed a brief account of our experience in our parish paper, to discover that several of my parishioners also had seen it. One lady, who attended the Wednesday morning Mass, mentioned that she not only had seen it on that Sunday, but also on the previous Saturday night and on both Monday and Tuesday—but always from a considerable distance. Needless to say, my wife and I resolved to go out that evening to watch. That night, we watched the sky for more than two hours, during which time planes constantly flew aimlessly back and forth—often as many as six were to be seen at one time, and always at least two. With such an inquisitive (or hostile?) reception prepared, there was no sign of the strange vehicle.

I heard of no further reports until about two weeks later, when four parishioners again spotted the craft over central Waukegan, just before an electrical storm moved in off the lake.

A flying saucer? It seems to me immaterial what you call it, but these facts seem obvious:

1. It was not any known craft.

2. It was manoeuverable, yet not powered by any conventional method, nor blown by the wind.

3. It was not towed by any other aircraft, and there were no aircraft in the vicinity at the time. Because it followed a zig-zag pattern, a tow craft would have had to be very close in order to reverse its direction and still have the towed object move smoothly and continuously while making the corner.

4. It could not have been a lighter-than-air craft. With compartments around the entire perimeter, there could not have been a sufficient volume for gas remaining in the centre.

5. It appeared to be intelligently controlled. Even coming in low, it easily cleared the electric high lines and maintained a safe altitude above the trees.

6. Its flight seemed purposeful, if for nothing more than sightseeing. The craft glided back and forth over the more densely populated communities and industrial areas strung along the lake shore and travelled as far west as U.S. Highway 41.

7. The flight appeared to be casual and unhurried. There was no apparent effort at concealment, nor was there any sign of hostility.

Where it was from, or why it was there remains a mystery.

We have wondered also about the darkened sections, the possibly unlighted compartments. Were they dark because it is easier to see out of a darkened room?

The Priest and the Saucer, by The Rev. Father R. Dean Johnson. From *Strange Fate*.

Let us assume for the moment that there are no such things as flying saucers. Is there any other explanation for the object seen by The Rev. Father R. Dean Johnson?

Many people claim to have made contact with the occupants of flying saucers. The best known was the late George Adamski. Less well known is Albert K. Bender. After being 'teleported' to a great cave hollowed out under the South Pole, the flying saucer crew's base of operations on Earth, Bender was taken on a tour of inspection. . . .

CAN YOU CONVINCE ME THAT
THIS ISN'T A DREAM?

I found myself in another semicircular room, though larger than the first. The walls were covered with glass screens of milky-white appearance similar to television picture tubes. The screens were divided by metal frameworks. In the centre of the room stood a circular dais on which I noted a slanted instrument panel containing many buttons and knobs, mounted on a metal pedestal. In front of the panel was a seat, for an operator not yet present. We walked to the centre of the room, stepped up onto the dais, and sat in a half circle of seats before the panel. Immediately the room began to grow dark, and from a sliding panel facing us on the opposite wall stepped a figure glimmering in a blue haze.

He was dressed in a uniform of golden colour. His silvery white hair contrasted with the skin of light brown colour. He appeared as if he might have a very heavy suntan. As he drew closer my attention focused on his face of handsome features. It was almost Earth-like, contrasted to the ugliness I had observed in the others. He was of muscular build and about nine feet tall. I gathered this was the 'exalted one' about which I had been informed, and that this bisexual entity was in charge of the base and probably the entire planetary operation.

The three men rose as he approached and I did likewise. They bowed as he stepped upon the dais. Each of my escorts then took a piece of metal, like mine (which I then discovered they were holding tightly in their hands), and in turn walked to the exalted one and pressed it to his forehead. I presumed I should do the same, and followed suit. When I touched his forehead with the metal I felt a tingling shock go through my arm, and into the temples of my head. The exalted one sat at the operator's position in front of the instrument panel and we also seated ourselves.

He turned, looked directly into my eyes, and I noticed that his eyes also glowed. Like those of the others, his eyes seemed to penetrate deep within me. Then he spoke to me without lip movement.

'I bid you a cordial welcome to our base of operations on your planet, and it is with deepest esteem that I permit you to be our honoured guest because you have given so much of your time to establishing friendly relationships with visitors from space. We knew of your activities long before you tried vainly to contact us with your experiment. Prior to our personal contact with you we had you watched. We were merely testing your sincerity.

'Having proven to us that you were a trustworthy person who had much will power, you, above anyone else, were chosen to visit with us and learn of our purpose here on your planet. You have already learned many things about us. You have listened courteously without troubling us with many questions, but I am certain you have many you would like to ask us, so we are now prepared to permit you to ask any questions you desire; but we must be free to decline to answer any we feel is out of order. May we now hear your questions?'

Here indeed was the moment I had awaited, an invitation to satisfy my curiosity upon so many points, and to hear the answers direct from the 'Head man' of the saucer people on Earth! Giving the matter quick but considerable thought, I decided I must ask questions of importance, for I didn't know how much time would be allotted for the interrogation. My first question came out without great hesitation:

'How long have you been on our planet?'

He answered unhesitantly, 'Since the year 1945 in your length of time.'

I continued, 'What is your main purpose in coming to our planet?'

'To obtain water from your vast bodies of sea.'

'For what purpose are you using this sea water?'

'We cannot answer that, but we have shown you what we do with it once we obtain it.'

'Do you intend to stay on our planet long?'

'Perhaps a period of fifteen of your planet years.'

'Do you make trips back and forth to your planet while you are here on Earth?'

He did not answer, 'Yes,' but replied, 'We have been changing our crews every two years.'

'I was told that you return some of the waste material from the sea water to the sea from which it came, but watching your process I did not see how this was done.'

'The waste is returned in the small craft that bring in the fresh supply. It is actually strewn while the craft is in flight.'

'Do you intend to cause any harm to our people while you are here?'

'We have found it necessary to frighten many, but we also have had to resort to graver action in some cases which involved deaths among your fellow Earthmen. We have carried off many of your people to our own planet for means of experimentation and also to place some of them on exhibit for our own people to see. We have specimens of peoples from many planets, but some of them do not live. These we preserve. Such has been the case of your Earth people; they have not survived.'

'Do you intend to take me to your planet at any time?'

'We would not take you to our planet unless you became an obstacle in our path; then we might find such action necessary.'

'Have I been an obstacle to you so far?'

'You have not done anything to harm us, but you have delved deep into the minds of our people by your determined initiative.'

'Why have you chosen me above some of our most brilliant men on our Earth?'

'Any person of high intellect or position in your society would not be satisfied with what we had shown or explained to him at this point. He would be inclined to keep the secret only until he was out of sight and then would have everyone out searching for us.'

'May I ask you some questions that have been puzzling me for many years, to which there is, of course, no true answer here on Earth as yet? Our scientists only surmise and guess as to these things and do not know for sure.'

'You may ask any questions you like, but I repeat, I will not answer if I feel I should not do so. Let us have some of these questions.'

'The big question I wish to ask first of all: How far does space extend? This is our biggest mystery.'

'You have chosen a very important question, and I feel you are clever for doing so. Space or the great void has no end as far as we have been able to explore. As we explained previously, there is a large main body from which all the planets and their suns are formed by means of being cast off into this vast void we call space. This main body seems to grow in size and never diminishes, despite the fact that it discards new bodies constantly. It is so hot a mass you could not go near it, even in terms of billions of your light years. All the bodies cast off are hot burning balls of fire, and as they reach the cooler parts of space they explode and form smaller bodies that circle them. These smaller bodies become planets as they cool off, but the cooling-off period consumes many, many years. We have sent out spacecraft to explore the regions beyond the circling bodies where there is an area that is deep black and in which you are unable to see anything. This vast black area is waiting for bodies to fill it. We have lost many of our exploring craft that went too far into the deep black and never returned.'

'Is there any possible way by which you can convince me that this is not just a dream. Can you, let us say, perform some kind of manoeuvre or make an appearance near my home which not only will make me realise that you actually exist, but will also demonstrate your reality to others who are sceptical about the existence of the flying saucers?'

'We can create an event that will prove this to you, but we do not wish you to tell others of its actual genesis. In a few days we will send one of our small craft into your area, where it will eject a fireball which will penetrate something of little value. We will not harm anyone, although it could cause a great deal of excitement in your community.'

'Will this occur near my home?'

'It will be near enough for you to hear about it and see the results.'

Suddenly the exalted one rose, and I knew that the interview had ended. He bade me farewell, and then each of the three escorts approached him and pressed their metal discs to his forehead. They said I should do likewise. The exalted one then left the room in the same manner as he had entered.

The three men guided me back to the monorail car and we retraced our route back to the small metal ramp where we had first entered the space ship. Although I am certain the temperature must have been extremely low, I did not feel any change of temperature. I did find myself clutching the piece of metal more tightly, and as I released the pressure lightly I immediately felt cold. The metal may have been a factor in keeping me immune to the low temperature—I never did think to ask questions about this.

As I descended a flight of metal steps onto the floor of the cavern, my three escorts suddenly halted me and again formed a circle around me. They held the pieces of metal to my head and I again lost consciousness.

When I regained my senses I was standing alone in the centre of my den. The headache remained, and my eyes burned and felt swollen. I sat down on the bed, rubbed my eyes and head. Again I wondered if I were going out of my mind. Had I suffered some kind of fit? Had I dreamed this and the other realistic experiences? I began to think it might be logical and wise to see a doctor.

Suddenly, I realised I no longer held the piece of metal, and my fears grew. Acting on impulse, I ran to the strongbox and opened it. There, at the bottom of the box, shining as before, lay the metal disc! I picked it up, and as I did so the pain over my eyes grew intense. As I replaced it in the box the pain went away. I locked the box again and went to my bed to lie down. As I did so I looked at the clock and noted it was four o'clock in the morning. I had been gone about six hours! Only a few hours remained before I must go to work, so I lay down and fell almost instantly asleep. A knocking at the door awakened me. My stepfather informed me I had overslept about twenty minutes and urged me to hurry.

As I went sleepily about doing my work, the idea of having dreamed the events of the past night continued to disturb me. Then I remember the promise I had exacted, that of some demonstration on the part of the visitors that would convince me, and possibly others, of their existence.

The proof was not long in coming. I learned about it on the morning of August 20th when a local paper carried the following story:

MYSTERY BLAST SHATTERS SIGN:
ORIGIN BAFFLES POLICE IN NEW HAVEN, CONN.

August 19th 1953—The city had a first-class mystery on its hands last night after a strange explosion at Middletown Avenue and Front Street tore a gaping hole in a metal signboard and brought reports of a flashing object heading towards East Rock at tree-top level. The loud blast occurred shortly after nine o'clock in the evening. Several residents of the neighbourhood, attracted to their windows and doors, reported seeing the flash of the explosion. Others said they saw a flashing object tear through the tree-tops and disappear in the direction of East Rock. Police admit they are baffled by the source of the explosion, other than it occurred in the vicinity of Front Street. But that it did occur they are positive. As evidence there is a large hole, about a foot in diameter, in a metal billboard at the corner of Front Street and Middletown Avenue. The object or projectile must have passed through the metal with great force, Lt. Raymond R. Coogan said. It made shreds of the sign arch, through which it passed, but left no powder marks or any tell-tale fragments that might give them a clue, Coogan said.

Henry L. Thalheimer, Chief Air Observer, said men on watch at the Ground Observation Post reported no unusual flashes or other unfamiliar sightings at the time of the explosion. Two aircraft were logged at two minutes past nine in the evening, he stated, but they were considered routine sightings.

Immediately after the explosion neighbours called the Fire Department and four pieces of apparatus responded and checked a gas station, adjoining the billboard but could find nothing suspicious. A check of homes and other buildings in the area failed to produce the source of the explosion.

The noise attracted a large throng to the scene. It was well past ten o'clock before the crowd dispersed and the traffic continued to flow smoothly on Middletown Avenue.

The neighbours looking to the police for an explanation shook their heads and retreated to their homes, when they were told the explosion and flash were still a mystery.

So went the article, which reassured me. True to their promise, the visitors had shot a fireball through the sign without harming anybody.
Flying Saucers and The Three Men, by Albert K. Bender.

Are Bender's writings nothing but science fiction? Did he suffer from hallucinations? Or do you think he really received visits from interplanetary beings who 'teleported' him to their hideout in Antarctica?

If flying saucers exist, where do they come from? It has been estimated that there are at least a hundred million inhabited planets strung out across the universe. Speculation is endless. . . .

Coral Lorenzen, Co-Founder of the world-renowned Aerial Phenomena Research Organisation has an intriguing theory . . .

FROM MARS WITH . . . ?

It would be impossible, in the course of years of close affiliation with the subject of UFOs not to have formed some definite opinions of my own concerning their origin. Much has been recorded and written about the elusive objects, and since the monumental works of the late astronomer M. K. Jessup many UFO researchers have gained a clearer picture of what the real answer may be. Jessup, an instructor in astronomy and mathematics at the University of Michigan and Drake University, compiled an impressive amount of UFO data in his book *The Case for the UFO*.

In the chapter 'The Incredible Decade', dealing with the period 1877–87, Jessup did a remarkably thorough search of astronomical journals for significant data. In addition to a large number of comets of unusual characteristics, reported by Jessup, three astronomical events which accompanied a veritable flurry of strange airborne objects within the earth's atmosphere suggested a fantastic theory to me. (1) One incident was the sudden appearance of a tiny companion crater to Hyginus on the moon. After no little disagreement among lunar astronomers who did not believe in changes on the moon, this tiny erratic was dubbed Hyginus N. (2) In 1878 a huge disturbance was noted in the atmosphere of Jupiter, the big-brother planet of our solar system. The storm, later to be known as the Great Red Spot, was peccan-shaped, between six and seven thousand miles wide, thirty thousand miles long, and it raced about the planet's atmosphere at a surface speed of approximately two hundred miles an hour, pushing aside all other surface features. (3) The most fascinating of these incidents was the sudden appearance of the two tiny moons of our sister planet Mars in 1877. Here are some curious facts about these satellites:

The great astronomers Herschel and Lasselle discovered the moons of Uranus through their powerful telescopes, but they never spotted the moons of Mars which, with the benefit of their instruments, should have been much less difficult to find than Uranus's satellites. The credit for the discovery of Deimos and Phobos, during the 1877 conjunction, goes to Asaph Hall. His find was verified by astronomers throughout the world, and they since have been successfully observed through smaller telescopes with much less power than the reflectors of Herschel and Lasselle. Why? Perhaps because they were not there before 1877! This is far more plausible than the assumption that they were entirely missed by the telescopes which had been used in a search for Martian moons in prior conjunctions. In fact, by 1862 it had been generally accepted by the astronomical world that Mars had no satellites. I am surprised that astronomy did not ring with the words 'strange things are happening' during that incredible decade.

The proximity of Deimos and Phobos to the surface of Mars, their small size and great speed, as well as their high degree of reflectivity, point to a strangeness which indicates artificiality. If these tiny moons are of the same degree of reflectivity as their parent planet, they are probably about five and ten miles in diameter, respectively. If they are metallic, they could be considerably smaller and yet highly reflective, so as to suggest larger sizes than they actually are. We can hardly deny the unusual brightness of these tiny bodies.

The Russian astronomer I. S. Shklovsky has pointed out that Phobos exhibits a strange acceleration during its orbit around Mars, which can be explained only if the satellite is a hollow sphere—an impossibility for a natural astronomical body. Shklovsky's theory that Deimos and Phobos are artificial satellites generally has been scoffed at, but nevertheless is a sound one, another instance in which prejudice replaces reason and logic; we cannot discard the facts.

Shklovsky and other Russian scientists further speculate that these artificial space platforms are evidence that Mars supports intelligent life—that, in fact, Mars became capable of space exploration and travel late in the last century. This certainly would explain the sighting of craft in the skies of earth during that incredible decade. However, other data must be discarded in order to accept *in toto* Shklovsky's theory of Martians with a technology only a few hundred years ahead of that of earth.

Shklovsky's theory would also appeal to a scientist with feelings of inferiority (an outstanding characteristic of the Russians) in the face of facts, such as those concerning the nature of Deimos and Phobos. Who can argue that it is not preferable to accept the existence of a species of space travellers only a century ahead of

A F F I D A V I T .

I, LUCAS EUGENE MEYER of 6 Witley Court, Moore Road, Durban, do make oath and say: -

1.

On Saturday, 31st July, 1954, at about 10.15 a.m. I observed an unidentified object in the sky moving slowly over the western suburbs of Durban.

2.

I watched this object for about ten minutes during which time I took three photographs of it.

3.

While I was preparing to take a fourth photograph the object vanished instantly.

4.

It was unlike any object I have previously seen in the sky.

SWORN to at Durban, Natal, this)
)
*8th.*day of October, 1954, the)
)
Deponent having acknowledged)
)
that he knows and understands)
)
the contents of this Affidavit.)

COMMISSIONER OF OATHS.

This sworn statement, by a man who had 'always been sceptical about flying saucers', describes the extra-ordinary events he experienced in 1954. Of the three photographs Mr Meyer took . . .

. . . this is the last, taken as the object was speeding
directly away from him.

Here is an even clearer picture taken in 1969, in England,
by Mr John Sanders but . . .

. . . however convincing it may look, this one has a much
more simple explanation!

earthmen in scientific achievement rather than a species hundreds and possibly thousands of years ahead of us?

If we consider the order of events by which space travel by man came about, and compare it with the facts available about UFOs, we must conclude that the intelligence inhabiting Mars has, in fact, been capable of space travel for a considerable period of time prior to the discovery of the Martian satellites. Earthmen first orbitted tiny objects and, as technology advanced, larger ones were launched. Eventually we hope to build a permanent space station at a convenient distance from earth which will facilitate the fuelling and launching of space ships bound for the moon and then the planets. However, if we can easily launch huge space ships, such as those seen throughout the years prior to the existence of the Martian satellites, why build small space stations comparatively close to our planet? The moons of Mars appeared in 1877, but astronomical records of unidentified aircraft predating those satellites by hundreds of years indicate that some intelligence has been capable of space flight for quite some time. Did these beings build the satellites (admittedly a gigantic engineering feat) to facilitate space travel? Hardly— they exhibited a great deal of talent in that direction before. Something was very busy in the solar system in 1877. The exact nature of those strange happenings is not precisely clear.

If, however, we postulate that several giant interstellar space ships arrived in this system in 1877, climaxing several hundred years of interstellar exploration by an advanced race, we at least have the beginnings of a workable theory which will explain in large part the strange happenings since 1877. Two such ships could establish powered orbits around the planet which had been explored and selected for colonisation (in this case, Mars) during previous surveys. This would also account for sightings of discs and cigar-shaped objects dating back five hundred or more years prior to 1877. After men and material were unloaded on the surface of Mars, the shells of the giant space arks may have been stabilised and left to orbit as a memorial to this gargantuan feat. Then, of course, depending on the needs of the visitors or colonists, they would set about adjusting to the surroundings or changing the surroundings to fit their needs. This would include a careful examination of the other planets in the solar system, possibly with an eye to the conscription of lower intelligences for labour purposes, etc. Bases could be established on the moons of the various planets to keep a close eye on the inhabitants and developments on the main planet.

At this juncture we must remember some strange new facts

about Mars which have come to light in our century. In 1952 Tsuneo Saheki, the famed Japanese astronomer and Mars expert, observed a strange 'explosion' on Mars, consisting of a brilliant flash of several-minutes duration followed by a luminous cloud. Saheki could offer no satisfactory explanation for the spectacle. Those he suggested but found inadequate, considering the characteristics of the phenomena, were: reflection from water (but there is no water on Mars); reflection from an ice-field (but ice does not form on the equator where the explosion was observed); impact of a meteor (which would have lasted only momentarily); an atomic explosion (but earthmen did not possess the capability to rocket an atomic warhead through millions of miles of space to Mars). One other possibility remained—a nuclear device had been detonated by the inhabitants of Mars. This, of course, was ruled out because it was not felt at the time that Mars could sustain intelligent life.

Times have changed, however. I quote from Space Handbook: *Astronautics and Its Applications*—a staff report of the Select Committee on Astronautics and Space Exploration to the Eighty-fifth Congress: 'Although human life could not survive (on Mars) without extensive local environmental modifications, the possibility of a self-sustaining colony is not ruled out.'

In April 1954 the *Australian Post* carried an article on space travel and quoted the famed Dr Girard de Vaucouleurs: 'We cannot doubt that there is something remarkable on Mars.' Indeed there is. Let's examine some of these:

On earth spring starts at the equator. On Mars it starts at the poles, moving towards the equator. In spring those strange Martian surface configurations, which have been dubbed 'canals', are the areas which become green first. This could indicate the presence of an intricate pumping system which utilises polar moisture. In 1952 a new green spot, the size of Texas, appeared. It became darker each year. It seems that some race with daring genius has undertaken a stupendous technological project. Our picture is almost complete.

Any individual curious enough to read this book is of course concerned with the intentions of our hypothetical race of inter-stellar pioneers. If he is a little fearful that is only normal, for the implications are fairly clear. But at the risk of seeming to soothe the reader I must explore the possibility that the examination and surveillance of the earth is only precautionary. There is a good deal of evidence to support this possibility.

America, the most advanced nation on earth, had not yet launched its industrial revolution at the time of the discovery of Deimos and Phobos. To advanced space travellers we would have seemed rather primitive. Therefore, only a cursory inspection was carried out periodically, possibly from a number of ships stationed on our moon—observational outposts. With powerful telescopes it would have been fairly easy to observe the burning cities of the Second World War, and by the time news of this holocaust had been relayed to headquarters on Mars, more attention would be concentrated on Planet III. The supposedly harmless race on earth would bear closer scrutiny, and the two atomic blasts of 1945 were easily detected. Knowledge of the discovery of nuclear fission by earth dwellers would be a growing concern for the colonists of Mars. Comparatively small in number, they would become preoccupied with our future scientific developments and military potential, and would begin methodical geographic mapping and military reconnaissance to determine the aggressive and defensive strength of the planet. They would be extremely interested in developments indicating our progress in space travel, for this could endanger their position in the solar system. A timetable of closer reconnaissance would be set up; thus we come to the pattern of visitations which have become obvious since 1947.

Every atomic installation, military base, and rocket launching station in the Western world has been visited by unconventional aerial objects during the past nineteen years. Information from behind the Iron Curtain indicates that Communist satellite nations have experienced similar visitations. Whenever a new military base is established or reactivated it is the subject of UFO visits. Mysterious, unidentified satellites have been observed circling the earth. Every time a major rocket launching is executed UFOs are there. Both prop-driven and jet planes have been paced by UFOs; some have mysteriously disappeared or crashed—specimens? Automobiles have been paced and even stopped by some mysterious method. People have been closely watched, approached—and there are thousands of mysterious disappearances of individuals in the United States alone each year—specimens?

Flying Saucers: The Startling Evidence of the Invasion from Outer Space, by Coral E. Lorenzen.

Many scientists believe Mars to be a dead planet with an almost total lack of water and a shortage of oxygen in the atmosphere. But is it? What are your opinions of Coral Lorenzen's theory that an alien race landed on Mars in 1877, quickly adapted to their new surroundings, and are now using the planet as a base for a systematic survey operation of our solar system?

You have now read some of the evidence for the existence of
UFOs. No doubt you have heard other reports of flying saucers.
Perhaps you have seen a saucer yourself, or know of someone who
has. Tell the class about your experiences.

But the UFO too has its critics . . .

THE CONTROVERSY

It all began on Tuesday, June 24th 1947. Kenneth Arnold,
owner of a fire control company in Boise, Idaho, was flying his
private plane above the Cascade Mountains of Washington.
Arnold is a handsome, athletic chap (former North Dakota all-
state football end) in his middle thirties, who uses his plane for
distributing his fire-fighting equipment. As he neared Mt. Rainier,
nine circular objects, in diagonal chain formation and moving at
high speed, passed within twenty-five miles of his plane. He
estimated their size as slightly smaller than a DC-4 which also
happened to be in the sky. They flew, he later wrote, 'as if they
were linked together,' swerving in and out of the high mountain
peaks with 'flipping, erratic movements'.

At Pendleton, Oregon, Arnold told a reporter that the objects
'flew like a saucer would if you skipped it across the water.'
Next day, the wire services blanketed the nation with the story,
using the word 'saucer' to describe the objects. Actually, Arnold's
original statement did not say the objects were saucer-shaped.
But the word caught on, and the mania was under way. Newspapers all over the country were swamped with phone calls from
excited people who had seen 'saucers' over their farms, towns,
and cities. Most of these stories were printed and put on the
wires with little or no checking. If the observer did not use the
word 'saucer', the local paper or press-service stringer put it in,
and if the wire story failed to mention 'saucer', papers receiving
it were likely to use the word in their headlines. In a few weeks,
saucers had been reported from every state in the union, as well
as Canada, Australia, England, and Iran.

Occasionally, sky objects of other shapes broke into the news.
There were balls of fire, ice cream cones, flying hub-caps,
doughnuts, and one wingless, cigar-shaped craft with rows of
lighted windows, long orange-red exhaust, and blue flames
dancing along the underbelly. David Lawrence, in his U.S.
News, disclosed that the saucers were secret U.S. aircraft,
'a combination of helicopter and a fast jet plane.' Walter Winchell
had inside information that the strange platters were from Russia.
Andrei Gromyko, in a rare burst of confidence, revealed that

possibly the saucers were coming from a Soviet discus thrower who didn't know his own strength.

Three military men lost their lives investigating the saucers. The first tragedy occurred shortly after the original sighting. A report reached Arnold that a weird doughnut-shaped craft had spewed forth large quantities of lava-like rock on Maury Island, a few miles off the coast near Tacoma, Washington. Arnold flew to Tacoma to investigate. On the way, incidentally, he spotted another cluster of about twenty-five small (two or three feet across), amber-coloured saucers.

The entire Maury Island episode later proved to be a hoax elaborately planned by two Tacoma men who hoped to sell the phoney yarn to an adventure magazine. Both men eventually made a full confession. Arnold, however, was completely taken in by the hoax, and his phone call to Air Force Intelligence, at Hamilton Field, California, brought two officers to the scene. On their way back, the left engine of the B-25 bomber they were flying burst into flames. Two enlisted men also in the plane parachuted to safety after being ordered to jump. Eleven minutes later the plane crashed and both officers were killed.

According to Arnold's several thud-and-blunder accounts of all this, the plane was carrying a corn-flakes box filled with samples of the mysterious lava. No trace of the box was reported found in the wreckage. 'Were both of these men dead long before their plane actually crashed and is that the reason their plane was under little or no control?' Arnold asks. In all his writings about the saucers he betrays this suspicion of mysterious forces and conspiracies thwarting his efforts to get at the real truth.

The second tragedy was perhaps the most dramatic event in the history of the saucer mania. It occurred in January 1948, at the Air Force base near Fort Knox, Kentucky. A round, white object spotted in the sky was chased by Captain Thomas F. Mantell, Jr., in a P-51 fighter plane. The object rose rapidly. Mantell followed it to eighteen thousand feet, then radioed to the ground, 'Going to twenty thousand feet. If no closer, will abandon chase.' That was the last message from him. Apparently he blacked out in the high altitude, and after reaching about thirty thousand feet the plane went into a fatal dive.

At first the military forces brushed aside the flying-saucer mania as mass delusion, but after the reports grew to vast proportions, the Air Force set up a 'Project Saucer' to make a careful investigation. After fifteen months they reported they had found no evidence which could not be explained as hoaxes, illusions, or misinterpretations of balloons and other familiar sky objects. Later, President Truman also issued an official denial that the military were working on any type of airborne craft which corresponded to saucer descriptions.

In February 1951, the Office of Naval Research distributed a ten-page report on the Navy's huge skyhook balloons, used for cosmic-ray research. The report pointed out in detail the ease with which these giant plastic bags—a hundred feet in diameter—could be mistaken for flying discs. The balloons reach a height of a hundred thousand feet, and are often borne by jetstream winds at speeds of more than two hundred miles per hour. If the observer guesses the balloon to be further away than it is, then, of course, estimates of speed can be incredibly high.

At a distance, a balloon loses entirely its three-dimensional spherical aspect. It takes on the appearance of a disc. From beneath, instruments hanging below the balloon's centre, can easily be mistaken for a 'hole', giving the disc the shape of a doughnut. If viewed from the side, the disc seems to be flying on edge, like a rolling wheel.

Through a telescope or binoculars, the flatness of a balloon is greatly magnified because of a curious optical illusion. A telescope does not present an image of the object as it would appear if you were closer to it. Instead, it takes the image, exactly as it appears in the distance, and enlarges it for the eye. You *seem* to be closer to it, but the perspective it would normally have if you *were* that close is not present at all. As a result, a globular object viewed through a telescope looks remarkably like a plate. If you have ever looked through binoculars at cars coming towards you on a long highway, you may recall how odd and flat the cars appear.

In addition, the plastic composition of a skyhook balloon offers a surface that seems highly metallic in reflected sunlight. Most of the saucer reports describe the discs as silvery in colour. At sunset the balloons may shine in the sky for thirty minutes after the earth has become dark. 'If your imagination soars,' the Navy release said, 'the light reflection from one side may impress you as the glow of an atomic engine. The wisp of the balloon's instrument-filled tail may impress you as the exhaust. The sun's rays may suffuse the plastic bag to a fiery glow.'

The first skyhooks were sent up in 1947, the year flying saucers were first reported. Arnold's original description of what he saw above the Cascade Mountains tallies remarkably well with what he would be expected to see had he flown near a group of smaller plastic balloons often used in place of a single large one. He estimated their size as smaller than a plane and the distance as about twenty-five miles—or twice the length of Manhattan Island. At this distance they would have been mere specks in the sky, and since Arnold was seeing them with unaided eyes, we cannot trust his guesses as to their actual size, shape, distance, or speed. Estimates of speed presuppose accurate knowledge of distance, and this in turn cannot be gauged unless the exact size is known.

Similarly, all the details of Captain Mantell's unfortunate death suggest he was chasing a skyhook. Moreover, it is known that such a balloon was in the area on the day he made his fatal climb. Even the descriptions of several hundred small 'saucers' which sailed over Farmington, New Mexico, on March 17th 1950, read like descriptions of balloons—though of course they could not have been skyhooks. They were white and round. They 'fluttered'. They seemed to 'play tag' with each other in the sky.

One of the few points on which all observers of flying saucers agree is that there is no noise. This excludes, of course, any known type of propulsion, but is precisely the way a balloon behaves. Observers have sometimes insisted that what they saw could not be a balloon because it was moving against the wind. They forget that wind directions in the stratosphere may be quite different from wind directions on the ground. At the time of the Navy's report, two hundred and seventy skyhooks had been released from various spots in the United States, often remaining in the sky more than thirty hours. Frequently, lost balloons were actually traced by following press reports of flying saucer sightings!

After the Navy's release on skyhooks, reports of flying saucers decreased markedly, and green fireballs, streaking across south-western skies, caught the public fancy. In the spring and summer of 1952, however, there was a new wave of saucer sightings, as well as a dramatic saucer scare in the nation's capital when mysterious blips of light kept appearing and vanishing on radar screens.

Many factors seem to be involved in the saucer mania. Although skyhook balloons, singly or in clusters, may account for most of the reliable reports, one must not forget that many other types of balloons are riding the skies. Weather balloons often carry steady or blinking lights and various shaped metal gadgets. Radar-target balloons trail large targets of aluminium foil. Guided missiles, and experimental aircraft of unusual design, may also account for some of the saucer sightings.

In addition, one must consider a score of possible illusions arising from faulty observations of planes, flying birds, the planet Venus, reflections of light on clouds, and similar phenomena. The theory that the discs are mirages produced by unusual weather conditions has been advanced by Donald H. Menzel, a Harvard professor of astrophysics, in his book *The Truth About Flying Saucers*. Normally such illusions would be rare, but under the pressure of mild mass hysteria, they greatly increase in number and, of course, are more likely to be reported. Even delusions without external cause can be induced in the minds of neurotics if there is a strong public belief with which the delusions may be identified.

Lastly, there are the lies and semi-lies. A book could be written about flying saucer hoaxes perpetrated in the past few years by pranksters, publicity seekers, and psychotics. Unfortunately, exposure of the hoax seldom catches up with the original story.

Even more difficult to expose are the semi-lies—accounts which have a basis in fact, but may be grossly exaggerated. For example, an observer sees a balloon but is convinced it is a saucer. Others are sceptical and this irritates him. So to convince them, he adds details, or exaggerates what he has seen. He may do this without being aware of it, and later recall the episode not as he saw it, but as he has added to it in his desire to convince himself and others. This is a well-known human failing and there is no reason to suppose it could not be involved in hundreds of so-called saucer sighting.

It is possible, of course, there may be some type of experimental aircraft resembling a disc and flying without sound that is still officially top-secret. But this seems extremely unlikely. Information now available on the cosmic ray balloons, together with the factors mentioned above, are sufficient to account for all that has happened. Official denials by the military and by the President have the earmarks of authenticity. Naturally, it will always be impossible to prove there *never* was a flying saucer. Believers in the elusive platters are likely to be around for decades. But there is every reason now to expect that the saucer mania will go down in history as merely one more example of a mass delusion.

Fads and Fallacies in the Name of Science, by Martin Gardner.

January 8th 1969 saw the publication of *The Scientific Study of Unidentified Flying Objects*, Project Director Dr Edward U. Condon. Completed in fifteen months at a cost of £208 000, the Condon Report was to be the U.S. Air Force's last word on the flying saucer, finding 'no direct evidence whatever of a convincing nature now existing for the claim that any UFOs represent spacecraft visiting Earth from another civilisation.'

Here is one of the fifty-nine detailed Case Studies from the Report. . . .

FLYING SAUCERS

CASE 29

North Eastern
Summer 1967
Investigators: Craig, Levine.

Abstract:

Six to sixteen bright lights, appearing and disappearing in sequence, were seen by several independent witnesses. Some witnesses reported seeing the outline of an object to which the lights were apparently attached. Investigation showed that the lights were ALA-17 flares dropped from a B-52 aircraft as part of an USAF aircrew training programme.

Background:

At least seventeen witnesses in ten independent groups reported seeing six to sixteen bright objects or as many lights associated with a single object, in the north-eastern sky at about half-past nine in the evening, EDT. Most of the reports indicated that the lights were visible for ten to fifteen seconds, although a few claimed durations up to five minutes.

The first report was made by a group of six teenagers who said they saw a noiseless 'flying saucer' with six yellow lights two hundred feet in the air over the concessions stand on the beach. They reported the object to be about twenty to thirty-five feet across with a 'round thing on the top and bottom'.

Publication of this report was followed by numerous reports of similar observations that had been made at the same time. These observations were from four different beaches, an airport, and a fishing boat off-shore. The reports varied in detail, but agreed that the sighting was sometime between a quarter past nine and a quarter to ten in the evening; several reports placed the time within five minutes of half past nine. They all agreed that the lights appeared in the north-east. Elevation angles that were indicated varied from five to thirty degrees above the horizon. The lights were described as blinking on and off; some descriptions indicated that they appeared in sequence from left to right and blinked off in reverse sequence, right to left. Most observers saw five or six yellow lights in a roughly horizontal line, each light being comparable in brightness with the planet Venus. One private pilot observing from the ground at an airport saw a horizontal string of six to eight pairs of lights, one yellow and one red light in each pair. The array moved towards the horizon and seemed to get larger for five to seven seconds, stopping four to five seconds, then beginning to retrace the approach path before blinking out about four seconds later. While most observers saw only lights, at least one witness, in addition to the teenagers at the original beach, reported seeing a large disc-like object encompassing the lights. Other of the witnesses 'had the feeling the lights were attached to an object.'

Investigation:

Six witnesses in this north-eastern area were interviewed directly, most of them at the locations from which they saw the lights. Others were contacted by telephone. The multiplicity of consistent reports indicated that unusual lights in the sky had indeed been seen; it was not certain whether they were separate lights or were lights on a single object.

Reports of these UFO sightings, when they had been telephoned to the nearest Air Force Base by observers, had been disregarded there. No unusual unidentified radar images had been recorded at the nearest FAA Centre.

The observations as described did not resemble air plane activity or meteorological or astronomical phenomena. No blimps or aircraft with lighted advertising signs were in the vicinity of the sighting at the time.

Since reports of UFO sightings had been frequent in this region, the investigating team spent several late hours observing the sky in hopes of getting first-hand information about the lights or objects that had been seen. No UFOs appeared during the watches.

One of the witnesses to the original sighting, a high-school senior, reported seeing 'that object' again on a subsequent evening. He guided the investigating team around a golf-course, describing a large saucer with surrounding windows which he had seen there just a few yards above his head. This report was judged to be a fabrication.

A few weeks after the project team returned to Colorado the NICAP Subcommittee Chairman, Raymond E. Fowler, learned that sixteen flares had been dropped at twenty-five minutes past nine EDT on the night in question from a B-52 aircraft twenty-five to thirty miles north-east of the beach area. Information about the flare drop was furnished, at Mr Fowler's request, by the Wing Information Officer.

The Strategic Air Command had initiated an aircrew training programme for dropping ALA-17 flares on the day before with aircrews releasing as many as sixteen flares per drop. The flares are released over controlled areas at twenty thousand feet or more

They burn with a brilliant white light, and are easily visible at distances in excess of thirty miles.

Conclusion:
In view of the close coincidence in time, location, direction, and appearance between the flares dropped and the UFOs sighted on the same day, it seems highly likely that the witnesses saw the flares and not unusual flying objects. It also seems highly likely that the suggestion of an outline of an object as reported by a few witnesses was, in fact, a product of their expectation to see lights in the sky *on* something rather than floating about by themselves.

> *The Scientific Study of Unidentified Flying Objects,*
> The Condon Report

But the ufologists were quick to refute Condon's findings. The most distinguished critic so far is Dr David Saunders, holder of degrees in chemistry and physics and a Ph.D. in psychology. His book *UFOs? Yes! Where the Condon Committee Went Wrong,* written in collaboration with R. Roger Harkins, ensures that the controversy will rage for many years to come.

Whether the UFO has any more reality than the werewolf or the vampire has yet to be proved conclusively, but of the estimated one hundred million inhabited planets it is not beyond the bounds of possibility to assume that many of these worlds support 'peoples' whose scientific achievements are far in advance of our own: races capable of reaching out beyond their own environment to explore the universe.

Can all the sightings be explained away as cosmic ray balloons, vitreous floaters in the eye, artificial satellites, meteors, marsh gas, sundogs, the planet Venus, ice crystals in the sky, lumps of decaying space debris, tanker planes refuelling, mirages, reflections of car headlights off clouds, hallucinations, or hoaxes? Or are our skies being patrolled by aliens from the stars?

YOU BE THE JUDGE